─────────── SECOND EDITION ───────────────────────────

PHYSIOLOGY OF AGING
A SYNOPSIS

SECOND EDITION

Physiology of Aging
A Synopsis

Richard A. Kenney, Ph.D.
Henry D. Fry Professor of Physiology
Chairman, Department of Physiology
George Washington University School of Medicine
  and Health Sciences
Washington, D.C.

YEAR BOOK MEDICAL PUBLISHERS, INC.
CHICAGO • LONDON • BOCA RATON

1   2   3   4   5   6   7   8   9   0   K   R   93   92   91   90   89

Library of Congress Cataloging-in-Publication Data

Kenney, Richard A.
  Physiology of aging.

  Includes bibliographies and index.
  1. Aging—Physiological aspects. 2. Age factors
in disease. I. Title. [DNLM: 1. Aging. WT 104 K36p]
QP86.K46 1989   612′.67   88-27639
ISBN 0-8151-5061-X

Sponsoring Editor: Kevin M. Kelly
Associate Managing Editor, Manuscript Services: Deborah Thorp
Production Project Manager: Nancy Baker
Proofroom Manager: Shirley E. Taylor

This book is dedicated to my wife,
BETTE, *for every possible reason.*

PREFACE
TO SECOND EDITION

The favorable reception that was accorded the first edition of *Physiology of Aging* has encouraged the writing of a revision. Some sections have been expanded and new illustrations and summary tables have been included. In recognition of the fact that many of the changes that occur with aging in apparently healthy individuals are profoundly influenced by life-style, emphasis has been shifted away from the notion of "normal" aging toward the description of "usual" alterations of function seen with the passage of years. The objectives of the text remain unchanged; in addition, it is hoped that this book might form a useful part of the preparation of candidates for board certification in geriatric medicine.

Richard A. Kenney, Ph.D.

PREFACE
TO THE FIRST EDITION

This book presumes its readers are already familiar with normal physiology, the focus of most "core" courses in the subject. It offers a concise description of the functional changes that occur as a part of the normal course of aging, and distinguishes these normal changes from specific pathologic processes that occur with increasing frequency as an individual ages.

With an increasing percentage of the population reaching old age, the health care practitioner must be able to recognize the changing parameters of health in the old and avoid the mistaken interpretation of these changes as disease. Some of the changes that occur are major and obvious; others are more subtle; and some can be slowed in their occurrence by an appropriate life-style.

Slowing those changes is both realistic and worthwhile, for the clock of biologic aging is not synchronized with the passage of years. It is the geriatrician's role to slow that clock relative to chronological time. To date, medicine has made enormous strides in adding years to life; the challenge for the future will be to add life to those years. Meeting that challenge requires an understanding of the special features of healthy function in this growing segment of society. The text that follows endeavors to stimulate that understanding.

In order to be concise I have been dogmatic, and only occasionally are statements supported by citation of the experimental evidence. Where specific data have been used in the construction of an illustration, appropriate reference is made. A list of suggested readings follows each chapter.

Richard A. Kenney, Ph.D.

——— ACKNOWLEDGMENTS ———

It is a pleasure to acknowledge the help that has been derived from discussions of this topic with colleagues, students, and friends of all ages. Helpful suggestions were also received from readers of the previous edition; many of these have been incorporated.

I am indebted to Linda J. Vaughan for the skilled and patient assistance that made the preparation of this manuscript a pleasure. My thanks go to Joumana Bizri and Kathleen Creel for secretarial support and to the editorial staff of Year Book Medical Publishers for their advice and encouragement.

Richard A. Kenney, Ph.D.

CONTENTS

PART ONE

General Aspects of Aging

1

Introduction

AGING IN MAN

Aging is a part of a continuum of changing function that begins at conception and is terminated by death. All too often, our interest is concentrated on just one part of this continuum—the adult years—so that differences in the function of the body in the years on either side of this central range come to be regarded as deviations from the normal rather than manifestations of a shifting state of normality. When we speak of a "physiology of aging," we are acknowledging that bodily function changes with the passage of years without there being any disease process involved. On the other hand, many disease processes profoundly affecting function show an increasing incidence with increasing age. Consequently, when one is confronted with a state of altered function, it is difficult to separate the two components: one the effect of aging per se (sometimes termed the "eugeric" process) and the other the effect of disease (or "pathogeric") process.

When we examine the continuum of changing function over the whole life span, it becomes apparent that, while some alterations have clear milestones (such as the ability to handle solid food, eruption of teeth, and menarche), other changes are much more subtle and extremely variable in their time of occurrence. The changes of aging fall into this latter group and, in contrast to the changes of function that are part of development and maturation, are typically decremental in nature, linear with time rather than "step functions."

Primitive man had very little chance of aging. Without the protections of a social organization and of technology, deterioration of physiologic function made him easy prey to a hostile environment. Failing vision, failing hearing, loss of teeth, and loss of muscular strength all worked together to make a long survival unlikely.

THE AGING POPULATION

There are presently more than 28 million people in the United States over the age of 65 years, rather more than 12% of the population. By the year 2000, the group will number 36 million and represent 15% of the population. Growth of this group has been dramatic in this century. In 1900, there were only 3 million individuals or 4% of the population over the age of 65 years.

Each day, 5,000 people reach the age of 65 years, and each day 3,600 over the age of 65 years die, providing a daily increase of 1,400, close to a half million each year.

The increased numbers of older persons in our society result from three factors: (1) high birth rates in the early years of this century, (2) large numbers of immigrants entering the society in the years between World War I and II, and (3) an increase in life expectancy.

As a description of the age profile of society, sociologists often use the "dependency ratio" of a population. This is calculated as the ratio of the sum of those younger than 19 years plus those older than 65 years to the number between these ages. The notion is that the latter group are "producers" of society's resources, while the young and the older are the "consumers." At present, the expanding older group is almost matched by a declining younger group so that the dependency ratio is projected to remain almost constant to the year 2010. In other words, as the demand for pediatricians diminishes, the need for geriatricians will increase.

HUMAN LIFE SPAN

Life expectancy has increased dramatically in this century. In 1900, only 39% of those born could be expected to reach the age of 65 years; today the figure is over 75%. Not only are more people reaching the age of 65 years, but once having reached that age, they live longer. Within the century, the over-65 age group has grown ninefold, while the over-85 group has increased 22-fold.

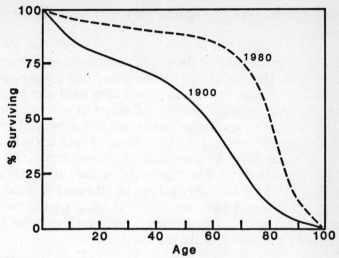

FIG 1–1.
The change in shape of the survivorship curve from 1900 to 1980.

A comparison of the survivorship curves for 1900 and 1980 reveals major changes (Fig 1–1). The substantial decrease in percent surviving that occurred in the early and middle years has largely disappeared. However, the extreme right-hand end of the curve has shown relatively little change. In other words, the prospect is not toward a population with growing numbers of centenarians but rather one of more and more persons moving more and more nearly toward what might seem to be their life span potential.

Viewed in the longer term, the effect is striking. At the start of the Christian era, the average age at death was probably around 30 years; at the start of this century it was 50 years; today it is close to 75 years, and yet those who survive the longest live no longer today than they did 2,000 years ago. (The Book of Joshua in the Bible states, "Moses was a hundred and twenty when he died; his eye was not dim nor his natural force abated.")

SEX DIFFERENTIAL OF LIFE SPAN

During this century there has been a change in the sex ratio of the population equally as dramatic as the change in life expectancy. There were 102 older men for 100 older women in 1900; today there are 150 older women for every 100 older men. In the over-75 age group, the ratio is 180 women for every 100 men, and this trend continues with further increments of age. Our aging society is becoming predominantly female.

This sexual differential is seen only in countries that are highly developed socioeconomically; developing nations show a symmetry of sexes at all ages. Hazzard (1986) has examined this phenomenon and reaches the conclusion that where health care need and health care resources are well matched, the sex difference in survivorship is accounted for in part by endocrine factors and in further part by differences in life-style. Both of these factors operate by delaying in the female the onset of major killer diseases such as atherosclerosis. An understanding of the details of this differential success in surviving will suggest ways in which male survival can be increased to match that of the female. This would have an enormous effect on the overall life expectancy of the population bringing it, in fact, close to the 85 years that some have postulated as the potential.

LIFE SPAN POTENTIAL

The survivorship curves suggest that the maximum achievable life span is a characteristic of the species and reflects a characteristic rate of aging. Cutler (1976) has studied the issue of maximal life span potential from an evolutionary point of view and has concluded that the rate of aging has remained essentially unchanged for the past 100,000 years.

The study of hominoid evolution suggests that over the course of 3 million years the potential life span has doubled. During this time, the rate of increase at first accelerated, but 100,000 years ago, the increase stopped and the potential life span became fixed. Brain size increased over a similar time course, and this has led to the notion that the brain plays some central role in the aging process.

It may be appropriate to specify in broad terms the different varieties of death that terminate the process of aging.

1. Trauma and accidents are the major causes of death in young adulthood. The rate of this premature loss is determined largely by the extent to which society will accept regulation to diminish the risks occasioned by, for example, high-speed vehicles, dangerous occupation, or life-shortening habits such as substance abuse or smoking.

2. Another cause is disease processes that have overwhelmed the defense or repair systems of the body. The past 100 years have seen a striking reduction in the number of deaths of this kind as understanding

of the basis of disease has developed and prevention and therapy have been instituted. It is probably not overly optimistic, therefore, to regard such deaths as "premature." Many diseases that led to death in the neonatal period have been conquered. Now the majority of deaths from disease occur in the elderly, in whom diminished functions can tolerate less accumulation of pathology than in the young. Some disease processes occur almost exclusively in the old, and this linkage of specific pathology and old age justifies the use of the term "pathogeric" to describe such processes. Nonetheless, deaths from pathogeric causes can properly be included in the category of preventable and, therefore, premature deaths.

3. If there were no deaths from trauma, and disease were totally eliminated, man would still die as a consequence of a reduced ability to maintain an equable internal environment in the face of external environmental stresses. This decreased ability to maintain homeostasis as one ages is universal. Since it involves no specific pathology, it can be called a "eugeric" change (leading to eugeric death). Paton (1954), in a delightful description of an individual in whom all the regulatory functions provided by the autonomic nervous system were blocked by the drug hexamethonium, speculated that death would ultimately come from increasing entropy of the unregulated system. Eugeric death and entropy have much in common. It might be assumed that the rates of failure of homeostatic competence would show a normal distribution, since many components of the regulatory complexes exhibit a linear decrease in function with age. On this basis, one might draw an ideal survivorship curve with a value of about 85 years as the mean age at death for those surviving accidental death (Fig 1–2). The concepts of "aging, natural death, and the compression of morbidity" have been reviewed by Fries (1980), who points out the implications of this changing pattern of survivorship for society, for research on aging, and for the practice of medicine.

This contention of Fries that man's maximum potential life span is immutable has come under vigorous attack on two major grounds: (1) it ignores scientific evidence gained in the experimental animal that life span can be extended by dietary restriction while maintaining good nutrition and (2) because, by suggesting that the task of the geriatrician is no more than rectangularizing the survivorship curve, it impedes research toward a larger goal.

Among the evidence neglected by Fries is the demography of the island of Okinawa. The Japanese dwelling in Okinawa are not genetically different from other Japanese, but centenarians are 30 to 40 times more common among them than in the population of the other islands.

Their diet is significantly lower in calories and significantly higher in quality. The incidence of age-related disease among them is deferred in time.

There have been reports of special groups of individuals who are exceptionally long lived. Claims of ages of 150 to 160 years have been made for groups in Ecuador and in Georgian Russia, but there are major doubts about the authenticity of these claims (Mazess and Forman, 1979).

Recently a technique of protein dating has been developed that will be useful to test such claims of longevity. It is based on the fact that amino acids once laid down in protein undergo a progressive racemization with time. While most proteins are dynamic throughout life with a recycling of amino acids, a few proteins, once laid down, do not undergo recycling. Tooth proteins and the protein of the lens of the eye are two examples. By estimating the degree of racemization of the amino acids in teeth that have been extracted or in a lens that has been removed because of a cataract, scientists may resolve the controversies presently surrounding the claims of great age.

The division of the population into "young," "adult," "middle-aged," and "old" is frequently based on personal stereotypes and is highly colored by one's own position on the scale. The World Health

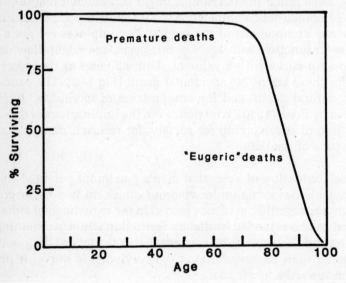

FIG 1–2.
An idealized survivorship curve in which randomly occurring death by accident is the only cause of premature death and deaths from old age are normally distributed about a mean age of 85 years.

Organization has developed a classification in which the "elderly" are those aged 60 to 75 years; the "old," aged 76 to 90 years; and the "very old," over age 90 years. This classification, however, has a limited value in describing the physiology of the process of aging, since as will be described, physiologic aging is a plastic process.

MAN AS A SPECIAL CASE OF AGING

In the vertebrate animals, a number of factors show some correlation with life span. There is an inverse correlation between life span and rate of metabolism, there is a direct correlation with the length of the growth period, and there is some direct correlation with body weight. On these bases, especially the latter, man appears to be an exception; his life span is longer than would be predicted. If brain weight is considered, however, the correlation improves, and man is no longer an exception. Conceivably, a large brain may make for an extended life span either by providing for a more effective, intelligent interaction with the environment or by providing more precise homeostatic control. However, there is no evidence that homeostatic control is any less precise in the chimpanzee than in man, and their life spans differ by a factor of two. Furthermore, the relatively strong correlation ($r = 0.80$) between life span and brain weight is not unique; the adrenal gland weight exhibits the same relationship.

Man is also an exception to the general rule in that his life span extends well beyond the reproductive period. This is not particularly advantageous from the viewpoint of evolutionary efficiency since it results in an increased drain on society's resources without a matching increase in the opportunity for species adaptation by genetic combination. Because a large brain does not make man more homeostatically efficient, its advantage must relate to the external rather than to the internal environment. The ability to accumulate information and communicate it within the species, which is provided by a large brain, justifies the long postreproductive life but does not explain how longevity is achieved.

THE STUDY OF AGING IN MAN

The study of the changes in physiology that occur with human aging is a difficult one. First, one must identify a population to be studied, and clearly the first criterion must be absence of disease. If the screening tests used to identify the disease-free population are too lax, pathologic changes in that population will be mistaken for physiologic. On the other hand, if the testing for the disease-free state is overrigorous, then the study population will consist of over-achievers, unusually healthy older individuals. Next, one must use informed volunteer subjects, and the invitation to participate may result in the recruitment of a group not representative of the whole; perhaps by being attractive to the unusually health-conscious individual or, on the other hand, the hypochondriac. Some studies have taken advantage of organized groups of one kind or another, students for example, or persons living in extended-care facilities. Such individuals by virtue of past or present life-style may not be representative of the open society situation.

The two basic experimental designs are the cross-sectional study and the longitudinal study. In the former, a population of a broad span of ages (perhaps birth to 90 years) is "sectioned" into narrow age-defined subsets and measurement made in identical fashion in each group. In the longitudinal study, a population is identified at an early age, and measurements are made on the group at specific time intervals so that the aging process can be studied in a dynamic fashion.

The cross-sectional study is open to error arising from the assumption that the 80-year olds in the study behaved, when they were 40, like the 40-year olds who were studied. This need not be the case, and this *cohort effect* arises from secular changes that occur in the population as a whole, over time. An example is stature (Fig 1–3). For a variety of reasons, some environmental, the height of 20-year olds in 1988 is greater than that of the 20-year-old in 1918. If there were no loss of stature with age, a cross-sectional study would lead to the erroneous conclusion that as individuals age, their height decreases. Another problem arises from differential survivorship by which only individuals who show (or lack) a particular characteristic survive to contribute to the later observations. To continue the example of stature, it is possible that tall, lean individuals tend to live longer than the short and obese; if true, this would bias the outcome of the study.

The longitudinal study shares the problem of differential survivorship and has the disadvantage of the time required for the study, which essentially amounts to the life span of the observer. Furthermore, it calls for a very stable and dedicated population.

A compromise between these two basic experimental designs is the semilongitudinal approach in which groups that overlap in age are studied for a limited number of years. Even so, secular changes in life-style, diet, smoking, and other habits can confound studies that extend over a period of years.

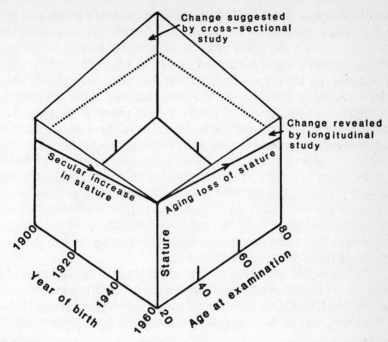

FIG 1–3.
The interaction of secular and aging changes as examined by cross-sectional and longitudinal studies.

Well-controlled studies performed on an appropriate subject population would ideally describe the eugeric process, providing information, for example, on the rate at which some aspect of bodily economy changes. But still, a further problem remains; namely that as individuals age, even from infancy onward, they tend to become less rather than more alike so that the average rate of aging change describes no more than what is "usual" under the circumstances of the study and certainly cannot be regarded as a "normal" value.

SUCCESSFUL AND UNSUCCESSFUL AGING

Rowe and Kahn (1987), in proposing the avoidance of the concept of "normal" aging, suggested that rather one should differentiate between individuals who age successfully, that is, show less than the usual decrement of function, and those who age less successfully and show more than the usual change. This concept is illustrated in Figure 1–4, which also serves to introduce the notion of functional age, the age at which an observed change usually appears in a population. This functional age is of use in describing an individual's status and could also serve as a quantitative measure of the effectiveness of interventions. The authors made the point that a major group of factors concerned in how successfully aging occurs are related to life-style.

Among the alterations in functions that have been clearly shown to be modified by life-style are the maximum rate of oxygen consumption, muscle power, speed of recovery from physical stress, and performance on a standard glucose tolerance test. These are all items that are commonly regarded as undergoing major age-dependent alterations. It is clear, however, when other variables are controlled, only a fraction of the change is purely age determined. The authors make the point that acceptance of the notion of successful aging can provide new directions to gerontological research and geriatric medicine in that effort can be directed more fully toward the identification of those aspects of life-style that make for success and consequently lead to the development of prophylactic gerontology.

The focus that society places on chronological age in terms of expectations of performance and the provision of benefits introduces what Alex Comfort has called "sociogenic aging." Individuals tend to behave in a fashion that society regards as appropriate for a certain age. The

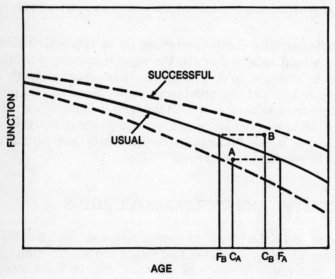

FIG 1–4.
The aging decrement of function. The *solid line* represents the "usual" change; the *dotted lines* the "successful" or "unsuccessful process." Also shown is the relationship of functional age (F_A, F_B) and chronological age (C_A, C_B) for individuals *A* and *B* who age at different rates.

person who, having reached aged 50 years, decides to give up singles tennis is likely to be responding more to society's expectations than to change in physical capability. For this reason and in this way, many of the beneficial aspects of the youthful life-style of regular exercise, dietary caution, and the like may be rejected, and aging thus becomes a vicious circle of positive feedback and progressive functional impairment.

SUGGESTED READING

Comfort A: *Aging: The Biology of Senescence.* New York, Elsevier North-Holland, Inc, 1978.

Cutler RG: Evolution of longevity in primates. *J Hum Evol* 1976; 5:169–202.

Economos AC: Brain-life span conjecture: A re-evaluation of the evidence. *Gerontology* 1980; 26:82–89.

Fries JF: Aging, natural death and the compression of morbidity. *N Engl J Med* 1980; 303:130–135.

Hazzard WR: Biological basis of the sex differential in longevity. *J Am Geron Soc* 1986; 34:455–471.

Kent S: The evolution of longevity. *Geriatrics* 1980; 35:98–104.

Mazess RB, Forman SH: Longevity and age exaggeration in Vilecbomba, Ecuador. *Gerontology* 1979; 34:94–98.

Paton WDM: Transmission and block in autonomic ganglia. *Pharmacol Rev* 1954; 6:66.

Rowe JW, Kahn RL: Human aging—usual and successful. *Science* 1987; 237:143–149.

Salthouse TA: Functional age, in Birren JE, Robinson PK, Livingston JE (eds): *Age, Health and Employment.* Englewood Cliffs, NJ, Prentice-Hall, 1987.

Walford RL: The extension of maximum life span. *Clin Geriatr Med* 1985; 1:29–35.

2

The Aging Process

Aging may be defined as the sum of all the changes that occur in man with the passage of time and lead to functional impairment and death. Bearing in mind that one can only describe a "usual" pattern of aging and that this pattern will probably change as life-styles alter, one may summarize the process by a diagram such as Figure 2–1. It can be seen that the changes tend to fall into three clusters: (1) some functions, typically those representing vegetative functions, that do not change; (2) a cluster dominated by reduction in active tissue mass; and (3) a cluster of "reserve" functions that show a major decline.

An alternative scheme of categorization of aging changes is as follows:

1. Those in which a function is totally lost, for example, reproductive capacity in women or the ability to hear sounds above a certain critical frequency.
2. Those in which change in function is accompanied by a loss of anatomical units with surviving units retaining the same functional capacity seen in youth. Examples are loss of nephrons in the kidney or loss of muscle fibers.
3. Those in which there is no loss of functional units but each unit operates at a reduced level of efficiency. The reduced conduction velocity of nerve fibers would be an example.
4. Secondary changes such as the increased circulating levels of the gonadotropic hormones when the feedback control exercised by the sex hormones is lost.

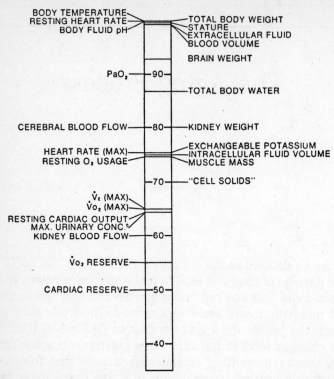

FIG 2–1.
Some anatomical and functional variables in a 70-year-old man, expressed as a percentage of values in the young adult. (From Kenney RA: Physiology of aging. *Clin Geriatr Med* 1985; 1:37–59. Used by permission.)

AGING AS AN IMPAIRMENT OF HOMEOSTASIS

To the physiologist, the state of health centers on the internal environment that provides the milieu for cellular activity and that serves as a buffer between the cells and the hostile external environment. Claude Bernard first drew attention to the "constancy of the internal environment," a concept that was later sophisticated by Walter Cannon in the term "homeostasis."

This state of relative constancy of the internal environment is all the time being challenged by the activity of the cells that it bathes and by external factors. It is defended by a host of regulatory systems that operate in a negative feedback arrangement. The pattern of this regulation is illustrated in Figure 2–2. It will be seen that, in essence, it consists of two concentric loops, one of which operates via the autonomic nervous and endocrine system. The second involves behavioral activity based on conscious information. Each loop contains sensors, a control center, and effectors. The control center serves as a comparator that compares the incoming information with a "target" value or "set point." Each element of the system is subject to aging change; the sensors may be reduced in numbers or in responsiveness; the center may lose its precision; effectors may become impaired. The end point of impairment is an internal environment that is incompatible with normal, healthy activity of cells and ultimately incompatible with life.

AGING AS AN IMMUNE PHENOMENON

The immune system, which is distributed throughout the body and interacts with all other systems, provides another aspect of defense of the internal environment. The immune system ages, and as it does so, immunologic efficiency decreases. As a consequence, there is an increasing incidence of infections, autoimmune diseases, and cancer. In addition, more subtle immune reactions may occur in a widespread fashion throughout the tissues, producing damage to blood vessels and parenchyma, which is expressed in a general impairment of function.

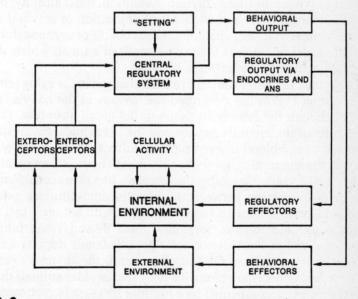

FIG 2–2.
The feedback loops that operate to produce homeostasis of the internal environment. *ANS*-autonomic nervous system. (From Kenney RA: Physiology of aging. *Clin Geriatr Med* 1985; 1:37–59. Used by permission.)

With increasing age, lymphoid tissue is lost from the thymus, spleen, lymph nodes, and bone marrow. In fact, the involution of the thymus gland, which begins in childhood, was noted by Galen as the earliest sign of aging. The loss of lymphoid tissue together with decreased vigor of the remaining stem cells reduces the cellular traffic of the immune system. Present evidence suggests that the major change in the system is in the T cells. This may involve the terminal differentiation of the T cells, which require thymic activity for their production from pre–T cells. Impairment of the terminal differentiation of the T cells may thus lead to an imbalance between effector and suppressor functions. Changes in the B cells, which are responsible for the humoral immune response, are smaller and generally secondary to changes in the T-cell population. Tests of T-cell function using hypersensitivity to antigens to which individuals have previously been sensitized have given equivocal results. However, the decline in function is more apparent in a test of delayed skin reaction to novel antigens or to challenge with tumor cells.

A number of immunologic models of aging have been proposed. One of these, put forward by Walford (1974), is the chronic graft vs. host reaction, which resembles the aging process in that both show depletion of lymphoid tissue, thymic involution, renal atrophy, occurrence of autoantibodies, and widespread deposition of amyloid material, which consists in large part of the light chains of immunoglobulin. A second model of aging is the thymectomized animal, which shows accelerated aging and a shortened life span.

The thymus is clearly central to all the changes in the aging immune system. Burnet (1970) has described the thymus as the body's "aging clock." Although the lymphoid tissue of the gland atrophies, the endocrine cells of the medulla remain and the hormone(s) thymosin can be detected in the blood of even old individuals. There is a profound decline in the circulating levels beginning at about puberty and continuing to age 50 years. Thereafter, the rate of decline slows considerably.

There is interaction between the hypothalamo-pituitary axis and the immune system. Growth hormone and insulin act on T-cell function; thyroxine and the sex hormones affect B- and T-cell function. Lesions localized in the anterior basal hypothalamus depress delayed hypersensitivity reactions. On the other hand, the thymus exerts an effect on other endocrine glands. In the experimental animal, the immune response is accompanied by a fourfold increase in corticosterone levels and by a significant but small rise in thyroxine levels. Since the glucocorticoids are immunosuppressive, this reaction may form a modulating feedback loop.

Evidence for a role for the immune system in aging is more convincing for the diseases of old age than for the normal process of aging. However, the theory that normal aging is the consequence of a developing immunodeficiency is attractive, since the process is potentially accessible to manipulation. Restriction of calories delays maturation of the immune system and also delays the decline in function. Administration of lymphoid tissue that is rich in mature T cells can extend threefold the life span of hypopituitary dwarf mice that are deficient in T cells. Fractions of the thymic hormone(s) can serve as "replacement therapy" for the involuted thymus. Valid though these two descriptions of the aging process may be, they are still superficial. Man is a complex machine that relies on the fundamental capabilities of the cell to perform metabolic exchanges of material, to synthesize specific large molecules, and to reproduce.

CELLULAR ASPECTS OF AGING

In considering the cellular aspects of aging, it is important to recall that the body contains several varieties of cells. First are cells that continue to divide throughout life, such as the basal cells of the epithelial surface of the body and the hemocytoblasts. These are referred to as "vegetative intermitotic" cells. Second are cells that continue to divide but differentiate at successive steps—"differentiating intermitotic" cells. Examples are the erythroblast and the spermatocyte. A third type is cells that are highly differentiated and normally do not undergo mitosis but may nevertheless be stimulated to divide when the need arises. This type of "postmitotic" cells is subclassified as "reverting"; an example is the hepatocyte. Finally, there are cells such as neurons and myocardial cells that are fixed in their "postmitotic" state and incapable of division. Life of the individual intermitotic cell is terminated by cell division; that of the postmitotic cell by senescence and cell death. Postmitotic cells vary widely in their life span; most neurons survive for the whole life span of the individual, whereas at the other end of the scale, the fully differentiated epithelial cells of the alimentary mucosa survive no longer than a few days.

Because of these profound differences among cells, it is possible to give only general descriptions of the signs of senescence in cells. In general, in the aging cell, the nucleus shows a clumping of chromatin, there is an increase in the number of nucleoli, and the nuclear membrane becomes invaginated. There is a reduction in the amount of rough endoplasmic reticulum, presumably concomitant with the lower synthetic activity of the aging cell. Changes have also been reported in the number and size of mitochondria, but the direction of change differs from tissue to tissue. More subtle changes in the mitochondria affect the pattern of the cristae. Typical of aging cells is the appearance of the chemically complex autofluorescent pigment lipofuscin. The pigment may be present in young cells, but the amount increases progressively with time, and the accumulation may be large enough to displace the nucleus. Although this pigment accumulation is a general phenomenon, there are differences among tissues. In skeletal muscle, for example, more lipofuscin is deposited in the muscles of the limbs than in the muscles of the trunk; in the adrenal cortex, there is a preferential accumulation in the zona reticularis. The pigment granules are possibly lysosomes engorged with fragments of membrane, degenerated mitochondria, and other organelles. At the ultrastructural level, the pigment displays a banded structure sometimes associated with crystalline material. Old pigment granules may also contain vacuoles. Although the chemical structure has not been defined, there is evidence that there are several, perhaps tissue-specific, varieties of lipofuscin. Although lipofuscin has generally been regarded as inert, it may nonetheless have a functional role. The concept of the accumulation of intracellular inert material gave rise at one time to the "clinker" theory of cellular aging in which the progressive occlusion of more and more of the cytoplasmic volume was the major metabolic depressant of the cell. On the other hand, the laying down of pigment may be protective to the cell in some fashion. In the central nervous system, pigment accumulation is found in areas other than those from which cells are lost.

THE STUDY OF CELLULAR AGING

Two major experimental models exist for the study of aging at the cellular level. One involves serial transplantation of tissues, such as the mammary gland, into isogeneric animals. Experiments of this type have demonstrated that the transplanted tissue may outlive by several times the original donor animal. Aging of a tissue may thus be more the consequence of the cellular environment than an inherent cellular property. The second approach to the longitudinal study of cellular aging involves the in vitro culture of intermitotic cells. The early studies of Alexis Carrel led to the belief that cells in culture were essentially immortal, but recent work has suggested that the periodic replacement of the culture medium in his experiments introduced new young cells to the population.

Work by Hayflick and his associates (1985) with human fibroblasts in culture has shown that diploid cells are capable of only a limited number of divisions before they enter a phase of extended and irregular cycles and finally die. Fibroblasts taken from a fetal (or young) donor go through an average of 50 doublings of cell number. Cultures from older donors have a reduced number, but there is a very poor correlation between donor age and the number of cell divisions. Cells taken from young individuals who suffer from progeria or other syndrome(s) of premature aging show a subnormal doubling capability. These fibroblast cultures also show an increase in latency—the period between the establishment of the culture and the outgrowth of daughter cells—with increasing age. The aging fibroblast cells become large and less motile and accumulate glycogen, lipids, and lysosomes; there is irregularity and prolongation of the prereplicative phases of the cell cycle. Cells may be rescued from senescence by transformation from the diploid character into a neoplastic cell line; in this condition, the cells appear to have an infinite capacity to proliferate. Transplanted into an animal host, such cells are commonly malignant.

The growth of a human fibroblast culture in the early phase of rapid doubling can be interrupted by cooling. On rewarming, the culture begins to double again; the process starts at the point in the doublings count where the interruption occurred, even though the imposed dormancy might have lasted for years. The sum of the doubling before and after the interruption is characteristic of that particular culture. This evidence suggests that under these conditions the aging and death of the cell are a programmed sequence brought about by specific aging genes. This is supported by evidence from cell fusion experiments in which "old" nuclei are transferred to "young" cytoplast, or vice versa. In these transfers, the nucleus is dominant; however, a senescent nucleus is recessive when fused with the cytoplast of a neoplastic cell line.

There is recent tissue culture evidence that the enzyme 5'-nucleotidase increases in concentration with each cell doubling, and the level may increase tenfold by the time the cells are senescent. No such increase in concentration was found in transformed cells that were capable of an unlimited life span in vitro. Measurements of 5'-nucleotidase concentration in bone have yielded much higher values in the adult than in the neonate. It is postulated that increased levels of this enzyme might limit the availability of nucleotidase for cell proliferation. The enzyme is responsible for the hydrolysis of adenosine monophosphate (AMP) and guanine monophosphate (GMP), and its increased concentration tends to prevent the reconversion of AMP to adenosine triphosphate (ATP) and thereby interferes with the energetics of the cell. There is also a link with an independent line of evidence concerning the role of nucleotidase in cellular aging. In spleen cells of mice and in human T-lymphocytes, the levels of cyclic AMP (cAMP) fall with increasing age while the levels of cyclic GMP rise. A similar change in the cAMP:cGMP ratio occurs in young individuals who have Down syndrome, which produces some signs of accelerated aging. Furthermore, antagonistic actions of these two cyclic nucleotides are known to be involved in regulatory actions at the cellular level, so that changes in their ratio may be a factor in functional decline.

These tissue culture experiments, while clearly pointing to a programmed and limited life span in the cultured cell, may have little bearing on the process of aging in vivo where the cellular environment not only is more complex but is also somewhat more plastic than the rigidly controlled culture medium.

THEORIES OF AGING

In all probability, man has speculated about aging ever since he became capable of abstract thought, and theories of aging have changed over the years in keeping with developments of biomedical science. Early theories focused on the notion of "wearing out" or exhaustion of some metabolic pool. Others focused on a rate of living concept and even led to the suggestion that man had a ration of heart beats (about 3×10^9) that could be used up either slowly or rapidly. In more recent times, aging of cells has been seen as the price of cell differentiation; as the consequence of switching on a specific "self-destruct" gene; or the action of a "killer hormone" that overdrives the cell to the point of exhaustion. Today, our theories are predictably based at the molecular level.

There is no a priori reason to believe that there is a unitary cause of aging or that individual cells age in the same way. It may be that each one has a mix of impairments at the cellular or tissue level and these all converge to the common end point of terminal dysfunction.

The work of Hayflick and his associates marked the start of intense investigation of cellular aging concentrating on biochemical processes.

The Error Theory

The error theory proposed that errors in protein synthesis arise at some stage in the transcription of information from the DNA template to RNA and the translation from RNA to the growing protein molecule. Some error in this chain or in the transfer RNA responsible for the delivery of the appropriate amino acid to the ribosome would produce an imperfect structural protein or enzyme. The longer the synthesis continued, the greater would be the chance of error or the more significant the error. The evidence at present is strongly against this theory. There is a strong fidelity in protein synthesis throughout life no matter how extended. Each day, the body for example, is called on to synthesize 8 g of hemoglobin; the structure of the hemoglobin of the centenarian is identical with that of the newborn.

Some enzymes do show signs of aging. Enzymes from an old person are more easily damaged by heat than those from the young; examples exist of the opposite being true. Differences of immunoreactivity exist between old and young enzymes. The evidence is that these differences do not arise from errors of synthesis but rather by a change in conformation of the molecule. Protein synthesis slows with age so that enzymes are not turned over so rapidly and therefore have a longer time available to undergo subtle conformational change. It should be stressed, however, that a majority of enzymes undergo no detectable age-related change.

Related to the error theory are two other theories involving DNA. One of these is often referred to as "redundancy failure." Gene sequences are repeated many times along the molecule, and some have suggested that only about 1% of the information carried by DNA is used by the cell; if error occurs in gene synthesis, there exists a backup of correct copies to replace the damaged one. As the cell ages, the supply of redundant genes is used up, and errors are then free to express themselves. In some cultured cells, a reduction in repetitive DNA sequences have been observed to accompany extended passage of the cell.

The second of these DNA-based theories postulates an impairment of the cell's ability to repair damaged DNA. When damage occurs by, for example, ultraviolet irradiation, the damaged segment of the DNA is excised enzymatically and a new segment inserted. Two lines of evidence support this relationship of repair to aging of cells: (1) the characteristic rate of DNA repair is related to the life span of a species, and (2) in cultured human cells, the rate of repair diminishes as the cells age. Again, were the cell not able to repair the damage, errors of synthesis would occur to the detriment of the cell's metabolism.

Free Radicals and Aging

A unitary approach to the problem of aging has been advanced by Harman (1968). His theory proposes free radicals as a central agent in the changes seen with aging at the tissue, cellular, and subcellular levels. Free radicals are chemical intermediates that contain an unpaired electron. These molecules are highly reactive and commonly have a brief half-life. Free radicals occur normally in metabolic reactions—for example, in reactions involving chains of enzymes. The superoxide radical O_2^- is generated by flavoprotein dehydrogenases and by mitochondria.

In the visual system, free radicals are involved in the transduction of light energy to the electric signal. The free radicals involved in normal metabolic processes form part of structured systems and are not free to diffuse within the cell. Diffusible free radicals can produce deleterious effects. They may be formed from materials in the diet or in the atmosphere, or they may be formed by irradiation with ultraviolet light. The important adverse reactions of these radicals are (1) destruction of thiol groups with effects on thiol-dependent enzymes, and (2) lipid peroxidation with effects on biologic membranes of mitochondria, lysosomes, and the plasma membrane. Lipid peroxidation leads to the production of malonic aldehyde, which reacts with protein to produce cross-links both within and between molecules. Malonic aldehyde also reacts with DNA such that free bases are liberated from the nucleotide.

Usually these effects express themselves as impaired information transfer in the cell, loss of specific membrane functions, impaired enzyme activity, formation of the membrane-based "aging pigment," and the cross-linking typical of aging collagen and elastin as well as reorganization of the mucopolysaccharides of connective tissue ground substance.

Cells protect themselves against the damage of free radicals by the enzymes superoxide dismutase and glutathione peroxidase as well as by compounds containing the thiol group.

There is some limited evidence that reactions producing free radicals increase with age, but there is no evidence of reduced activity of superoxide dismutase or glutathione peroxidase. There is evidence, on the other hand, that the efficiency of this natural scavenging system can be enhanced by exercise of the endurance type.

A major attraction of the free radical theory of aging is that it makes aging potentially treatable. There are substantial sales of vitamin E and vitamin C for their antioxidant properties. Butylated hydroxytoluene (BHT), a food additive used to retard rancidity, has also been promoted as a drug for this purpose. Some animal experiments have extended the life span by incorporating an antioxidant into the diet. A Rumanian study, which has not been successfully repeated, showed some improved survival of elderly individuals who took vitamin E. Other experiments have suggested that antioxidants are effective only when the conditions of the experiment tend to shorten the life span of control animals. Still other studies have shown no effect on the rate of aging or on the life span.

A number of proposals have been made as alternatives to the central role of antioxidants in retarding cellular aging in an attempt to explain observations in which the life span of treated animals was increased. Some of the proposed mechanisms are the following:

1. Antioxidants depress appetite, reduce food intake, and thus delay growth and maturation and lengthen life span.
2. Antioxidants suppress tumor growth, which is commonly the cause of death in longevity studies.
3. Antioxidants retard the aging decline of immune processes.

Clearly, at present we have in our hands only a few fragments of the picture of cellular aging.

SUGGESTED READING

Adelman RC, Roch GS (eds): *Testing the Theories of Aging*, Boca Raton, Fla., CRC Press, 1982.

Burnet FM: An immunological approach to aging, *Lancet* 1970; 2:358.

Goldstein AL, Thurman GB, Low TLK, et al: Thymosin: The endocrine thymus and its role in the aging process, in Cherkin A, et al (eds): *Physiology and Cell Biology of Aging*. New York, Raven Press, 1979.

Harman D: Free radical theory of aging: Effect of free radical inhibitors on the mortality rate of LAF_1, Mice. *Gerontology* 1968; 23:476.

Hayflick L: The cell biology of aging. *Clin Geriatr Med* 1985; 1:15–27.

Rothstein M: Biochemical studies of aging. *C and EN*, Special Report, August 1986, pp 26–39.

Strehler BL: Aging at the Cellular Level, in Rossman I, (ed): *Clinical Geriatrics*. Philadelphia, JB Lippincott, Co, 1971.

Sun AS, Aggarwal BB, Packer L: Enzyme levels of normal human cells: Aging in culture, *Arch Biochem Biophys* 1975; 170:1.

Walford RL: Immunological theory of aging: Current status. *Fed Proc* 1974; 33:2020.

3

Aging Changes in Body Conformation and Composition

The fundamental changes of aging occur at the cellular and subcellular levels and express themselves not only in altered function but also in a changed gross anatomy. Major signs of aging are seen in both body conformation and composition.

BODY CONFORMATION

Most anthropometric studies have been of the cross-sectional type. As we have seen, such studies are likely to be misleading because of secular changes, for example, those that have occurred in stature over the years. Studies performed in this fashion have revealed an apparent loss of height with aging, that begins at 30 years of age and progresses at a rate of 1 cm per decade thereafter.

Remeasurement studies of the longitudinal or semilongitudinal type show variability in the age of onset of loss of stature and a rate of loss only half of that suggested by cross-sectional studies. Some studies, for example, reveal a gain in height continuing into the 40s before any decline begins. This "late growth" has been attributed to the development of a more erect posture coupled with some continued growth of the vertebrae. Measurements of sitting height suggest that the loss of stature is almost equally divided between trunk and legs. However, shrinkage does not occur simultaneously in these two components: loss of leg length precedes shortening of the trunk. The length of the femur shows almost no age-related change and a significant part of the reduction in standing height must be produced by changes in the joints and by a flattening of the foot arches. The components of loss of trunk length are an increase in spinal curvatures and some compaction of the intervertebral discs. Arm span changes little if at all with aging, so the stature that had been attained at maturity can be estimated in old age from the span.

Shoulder width diminishes with age in both sexes, and this is due mostly to loss of muscle mass in the deltoids; in both sexes, pelvic diameter increases. The chest circumference increases as aging of the lung reduces the inwardly directed elastic force that the lung exerts on the chest wall. Most of the increase in circumference comes about by change in the anterior-posterior diameter. In the very old, the lateral diameter of the chest may diminish when loss of bone mineral from the ribs weakens them to the point where they no longer support the force of the intercostal muscle and the lower thorax becomes "pinched."

The depth of the abdomen measured in the supine position increases rather steadily from about age 25 years onward; the increase amounts to about 3 cm by the age of 70 years and tends to be larger in the female than in the male. The reverse is true of the anterior-posterior chest diameter. Circumference of the head diminishes a little up to the age of 60 years, due mostly to the loss of subcutaneous tissue, and then re-enlarges back to, or beyond, the youthful size as bone continues to be laid down on the skull. The nose and ears continue to grow in length well past maturity; the nose broadens, and the ear lobes thicken.

In men, body weight tends to increase to the late 50s and then decline at a rate that accelerates in the 60s and 70s. In women, body weight continues to increase into the 60s before showing a decline that is then less obvious than in the male. The increase in body weight in middle age (the "middle-aged spread"), which is regarded as usual in our society, is mainly the result of an inactive life-style in an environment where food is plentiful. This "aging" change does not appear in more primitive or less fortunate societies.

BODY COMPOSITION

The gross composition of the body may be studied by several non-invasive means. Measurement of *total body water* by an indicator dilution method provides an index of the adiposity of the body, since fat contains very little intracellular or extracellular water. Another approach to determining adiposity depends on the fact that fat is the only

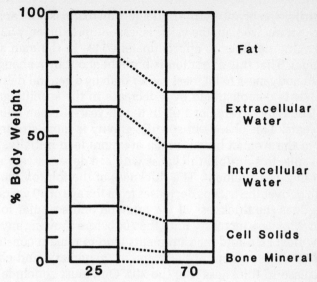

FIG 3–1.
Typical proximate composition of men at ages 25 and 70 years. Note especially the changing ratio of intracellular and extracellular water.

component of the body that is lighter than water. Measurement of *specific gravity*, by weighing an individual in air and in water, provides a moderately reliable index of the relative contribution of adipose tissue to body weight. Assessment of the amount of subcutaneous fat is made by measuring the *skin-fold thickness* at selected sites. Measurements of adiposity by one of these means lead to the concept of *fat-free mass* or *lean body mass*. The former measures all the fat-free substances of the body, whereas the latter includes the structural lipid substances.

An alternative concept is the *body cell mass*, which is defined as the mass that uses oxygen; it includes muscle and the parenchymal cells but excludes the dense supporting tissues such as bone and cartilage. Since cells typically have a high potassium content while the extracellular material contains very little, body cell mass may be estimated from the size of the pool of exchangeable potassium measured by diluting the isotope ^{42}K. Since some part of the pool of body potassium exchanges only very slowly, or in fact, is nonaccessible, a preferred measurement involves whole-body counting of the naturally occurring ^{40}K.

At any age, there is a wide variation among individuals in body weight, the fraction contributed by fat, and the total volume of body water (Fig 3–1). In an "average" young man, (one neither strikingly lean nor obviously obese), the totally body water measured as the volume of distribution of antipyrine or deuterium oxide is 60% of the body weight; in a young woman, the value is less—approximately 52%. With aging, the value declines to approximately 54% in the man and 46% in the woman. That this alteration is brought about by a change in the ratio of lean body mass to fat mass rather than by a general dehydration of the tissues is demonstrated by a decrease in the specific gravity of the body. The typical value of 1.08 in the 30-year-old man falls to 1.03 at age 70 years. This change in specific gravity is more striking in the man than in the woman because men are more lean initially.

The change in skin-fold thickness with age depends very much on the site of the measurement. The thickness of the fold on the dorsum of the hand or over the triceps decreases from the age of 50 years onward in men as does the thickness of the humeral and scapular folds. Paraumbilical thickness increases until the 70s before showing any decline. In women, most skin-fold measurements tend to remain constant until the age of 65 years, except at the scapular, mammary, and chin sites, which increase in thickness into the 70s. One must conclude that the greater part of the extra adipose tissue in the aged person is laid down internally, within organs, in the mesentery or perinephric areas rather than in the subcutaneous sites.

The two major divisions of body water, intracellular and extracellular fluids, do not diminish equally with age. In the young adult, the volumes of these components have a ratio of 2:1. The reduction in fluid volume that occurs with age is more marked in the intracellular than in the extracellular spaces, so that the ratio becomes less than 2:1, tending toward the values seen in the preadolescent. This change could reflect either a dehydration of the cells or a loss of cell mass with maintained hydration.

Estimates of the cell mass of the body made either by measuring exchangeable potassium or by the preferred procedure of whole-body counting of ^{40}K reveal a reduction of cell mass relative to body weight. In men, total body potassium decreases from a value of 54 mEq/kg of body weight at age 40 years to 50 mEq/kg at age 70 years. There is a similar percent change in women, but absolute values are lower by approximately 8 mEq/kg of body weight.

Although most of the loss of lean body mass occurs in muscle, virtually all organs participate in this age-related loss of mass, though to varying degrees. On the one hand, the lungs show no loss of weight or, in fact, may show an increase; on the other, the liver and kidneys lose a third of their weight between ages 30 and 90 years. An exception to this pattern of loss is the prostate, which doubles in weight between youth and old age.

Just as potassium can be used as a marker of the intracellular space, exchangeable sodium (Na^+_e) can be used as a marker of the extracellular. Between ages 30 and 60 years, the ratio $Na_e:K_e$ rises from 1.0:1 to 1.2:1 (Fig 3–2). These studies are in agreement with direct analysis of muscle and visceral tissues in demonstrating a shift in favor of extracellular components with aging. Most studies of humans in this area have been of the cross-sectional type, but the relatively few remeasurement studies have produced essentially the same picture.

SUMMARY

In summary, with increasing age, a small loss of height, a modest loss of weight, a small consequent loss of body surface area, and a significant loss of active cell mass occur. In the old person, the body is housing a smaller engine. It is important to keep this in mind when considering the decline of function with age. Common measurements of functions such as metabolic rate, the rate of glomerular filtration or perfusion of the kidney, and cardiac output are all standardized for comparison of one individual with another or for comparison with a normal value for a given surface area. This places the old individual

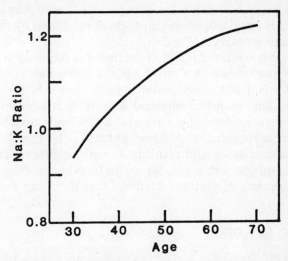

FIG 3–2.
The changing ratio of exchangeable Na^+ and K^+. (Based on data from MacGillivray I, Buchanan TJ, Billewicz WZ: *Clin Sci* 1960; 19:17–25.

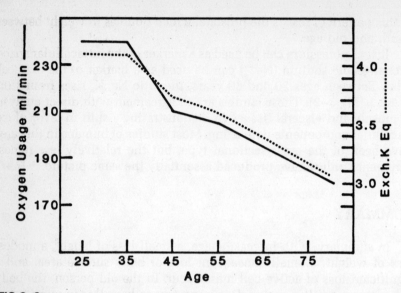

FIG 3–3.
The similar courses of the changes in basal oxygen consumption and in exchangeable K+ content.

at a disadvantage and may obscure the fact that a reduced function might be appropriate for the decreased tissue mass it serves. For example, the resting rate of oxygen consumption declines significantly between ages 30 and 70 years, but this decline does not appear when the rate of use is standardized to cell mass as estimated by the amount of exchangeable potassium (Fig 3–3).

However, this notion of function declining in harmony with a mass with diminishing metabolism raises again a fundamental question of aging—how far is decline inevitable? Muscle mass is better conserved in individuals who maintain physical activity. It is highly likely that changes in the quality and character of the diet could also have a role in maintaining a youthful ratio of lean to fat. It is far from certain that such life-style changes would result in an equal conservation of functions, cardiorespiratory or renal, for example, which service the body mass. Is a "harmony of decline" designed into the aging process?

SUGGESTED READING

Boddy K, King PC, Womersley J, et al: Body potassium and fat-free mass. *Clin Sci* 1973; 44:622–625.

Damon A, Seltzer CC, Stoudt HW, et al: Age and physique in healthy white veterans at Boston. *Aging Hum* 1972; 3:202–208.

Durnin JVGA, Womersley J: Body fat assessed from total body density and its estimation from skin fold thickness: Measurement on 481 men and women aged from 16 to 72 years. *Br J Nutr* 1974; 32:77–79.

Forbes GB: The adult decline in lean body mass. *Hum Biol* 1976; 48:161–173.

Lye M: Distribution of body potassium in healthy elderly subjects. *Gerontology* 1981; 27:286–292.

MacGillivray I, Buchanan TJ, Billewicz WZ: Values for total exchangeable sodium and potassium in normal females based on weight, height and age. *Clin Sci* 1960; 19:17–25.

Miall WE, Ashcroft MT, Lovell HG, et al: A longitudinal study of the decline of adult height with age in two Welsh communities. *Hum Biol* 1967; 39:445–454.

Moore F, Olesen KH, McMurrey JD, et al: *The Body Cell Mass and Its Supporting Environment.* Philadelphia, WB Saunders Co, 1963.

Novak LP: Aging, total body potassium, fat free mass and cell mass in males and females between ages 18 and 85 years. *Gerontology* 1972; 27:438–443.

Rossman IL: Anatomic and body composition changes with aging, in Finch CE, Hayflick L (eds): *Handbook of the Biology of Aging.* New York, Van Nostrand Reinhold Co, 1977.

PART TWO

Aging of Tissues and Organ Systems

4

Blood, Supporting Tissues, Muscle, Skin, and Teeth

BLOOD

The red blood cells show morphological and biochemical changes as they age, which ultimately results in their removal from the circulation after a life span of 120 days. Aging cells lose potassium, become increasingly dense, and are increasingly fragile to mechanical or osmotic challenge. The red blood cells of old individuals show only subtle differences from those of young persons. There is a small increase in mean cell diameter and mean corpuscular volume and also an increase in fragility measured in terms of the tonicity that produces 50% hemolysis. In old persons, there is also increased variability of the cell fragility. This age-related change may be due to a change in the relationship of volume to surface area of the average cell, or it may reflect a decrease in the efficiency of the spleen and lymphoid tissue to remove aged cells. Estimations of the life span of red blood cells, however, show this to be essentially the same in the old person as in the young.

The blood volume is well maintained in persons until they reach approximately 80 years of age. Up to this time, the ratio of blood volume to active tissue mass increases. In healthy individuals, the red blood cell count, hematocrit value, and hemoglobin concentration remain within the normal range to age 65 years; thereafter, there may be a slight decrease. It seems likely that a major cause of the relatively high incidence of anemia in old persons reported in hospital surveys is chronic disease, with some contribution from suboptimal nutrition as a result of poverty, lack of mobility, or decreased interest in food. The erythrocyte sedimentation rate is increased in the old, probably as a result of changes in the plasma protein concentrations, especially that of fibrinogen. A small increase in viscosity is seen in older men, perhaps again, due to the increased fibrinogen concentration. Few significant morphological changes occur in the white blood cells. Granulocytes show increased lobulation and reduced granulation; their osmotic resistance increases. Lymphocyte production is reduced, but there is an increased concentration of RNA in the cell. Platelet count and function remain unchanged.

Plasma protein concentrations decrease with age, due mainly to a reduction in the albumin fraction. There is a small rise in the globulin fraction. As a consequence, the albumin/globulin ratio falls and the colloid osmotic pressure is reduced. The fibrinogen concentration rises by approximately 25% between ages 30 and 70 years. This appears to be the only change in the clotting factors.

High density lipoprotein (HDL) concentrations are equal between the sexes until puberty. In the female, the concentration rises until age 70 years; in the male, the value after puberty remains relatively constant but begins to rise toward the female value around the age of 50 years. Low density lipoprotein (LDL) concentrations in both sexes rise through adulthood, but the female value rises beyond the male at the time of menopause. The ratio LDL/HDL, which is favored as a single index of atherogenic risk, is higher in males throughout life, although there is some convergence of values in late middle age.

There is no age-related change in plasma osmotic pressure and only minor alterations in the chemical composition of the plasma. The level of ionized calcium shows a slight decrease; the plasma bicarbonate level falls at a rate of approximately 1% per decade from age 50 years onward. Since the arterial blood PCO_2 remains stable in the absence of respiratory dysfunction, the pH falls from the young adult value of 7.40 to 7.38 in old age. The plasma concentrations of nitrogenous metabolites, urea, uric acid, and creatinine rise as renal function declines with age.

The amount of active red bone marrow diminishes with age, being replaced by yellow marrow. The loss occurs first in the long bones and more slowly in the flat bones. There is very little reduction in the level of vertebral red bone marrow. The cytologic characteristics of the remaining red marrow are the same as in the young.

The functional reserve for hematopoiesis—that is, the ability to accelerate the production of red blood cells and to convert yellow bone marrow to the red, cell-producing variety when challenged by a need to replace lost cells—is reduced in the elderly, but in practice, the response to hemorrhage, although slow, remains adequate.

SUPPORTING TISSUES

With aging, there is a relative increase in the size of the extracellular component of body water. This water is distributed among the solid and semisolid components of the extracellular material that make up the supporting tissues of the body, the connective tissue, cartilage and bone. These tissues are characterized by the very high proportion of material that is extracellular.

Connective Tissue

Throughout life, the supporting matrix changes. In the infant, it is a highly aqueous environment for the cells. As the tissue matures, there is a decrease in the amount of water and an increase in the solid components. Typically, these solid materials are polymers that are more condensed as the tissues age. Connective tissue has two major components: ground substance, which consists of mucopolysaccharides in the form of a hydrated gel, and fibrous proteins, collagen, elastin, and reticular fibers. These substances are synthesized by fibroblasts.

Ground substance differs from one location to another depending on the function that needs to be served. In tissues that require mobility, the major component is hyaluronic acid; in tissues that need mechanical support and firmness, chondroitin sulfate is found.

Intermediate between ground substance and the fibrous elements of connective tissue is basement membrane, which consists of glycoprotein organized in a fine fibrillary form. The basement membrane defines the boundary between epithelial or endothelial tissues and connective tissue. It is thus a barrier that must be crossed twice by material in transit between blood and cell.

The age-related changes in ground substance are essentially part of the process of maturation, with an increase in the density of the gel and loss of water. The volume occupied by ground substance is reduced as the fiber density increases.

Diffusion of material within the extracellular component is potentially impaired with age, and cell mobility is reduced. These changes threaten both the nutrition of cells and the repair and healing process.

Collagen is formed by the aggregation of molecules of tropocollagen. The aggregation occurs both end-to-end and side-to-side. The molecules of tropocollagen are staggered in the side-by-side relationship by one quarter of the long dimension. This produces the characteristic cross-banding of the collagen fibers at the periodicity of 6,400 A. As the tissue matures and ages, collagen fibers increase in number and in size. Cross-linkage develops between fibers. The solubility of the collagen is reduced, and the structure becomes more stable. This reduced rate of turnover is evidenced by reduced excretion in the aged of hydroxy-proline, the marker amino acid of collagen. The mechanical properties of the fibers change; greater force is required to produce a given degree of extension, and once stretched, the fibers only slowly return to their original length (hysteresis).

In extreme old age, there is an increase in the concentration of the enzyme collagenase. The phase of increasing rigidity of the tissue matrix is thus followed by a phase of weakening.

Fibers of elastin also develop cross-linkages as they age; water is lost, and the fibers become more intensely yellow. The fibers become more rigid and, under continued stress, tend to fray and fragment. In some cases, the lost elastic fibers are replaced by collagen.

The delicate reticular fibers of connective tissue are abundant in the young but with maturation of the tissue are replaced by fibers of collagen.

Aging is also associated with the appearance of a fourth fiber element, pseudoelastin. Chemically, it is intermediate in composition between collagen and elastin. Structurally, it appears to consist of collagen with a coat of amorphous material, which masks the typical cross-banding of collagen.

Cartilage

Hyaline cartilage dehydrates as it ages and is converted to fibrocartilage. The articular cartilage, which in the young person is translucent, becomes opaque and yellow with age; elasticity is lost, and the cartilage thins in weight-bearing areas—for example, the menisci of the knee joint. In both connective tissue and cartilage, the increasing fiber density provides nidi for the deposition of bone mineral. Calcification occurs in the major blood vessels; cartilage may be converted to true bone.

The effects of aging changes in the connective tissue are global. Skin loses its elasticity and wrinkles, joints become stiffened by the increase in fibrous tissue around them, lungs lose their elastic recoil, and costal cartilages become increasingly rigid. Loss of hydration in the nucleus pulposus of the intervertebral disks leads to compaction of the vertebrae and shrinkage in stature. The cardiovascular system, which depends to a great extent on the properties of distensibility and elasticity, is greatly impaired as the matrix changes. The chambers of the heart become less distensible, and as a consequence, there is less contractility; the elastic arteries become more rigid and lose their "windkessel" function; valves stiffen, and even the pacemaker cells of the nodal tissue may be displaced by collagen fibers.

Bone

Although the tendency in the fibrous tissue is for calcium to be deposited, bone loses mineral as it ages. The development of this osteoporosis involves a loss of as much as 10% of the bone salts. In the long bones, the net loss of mineral is associated with remodeling. The bone erodes from within, while deposition is occurring at a slower rate at the periosteal surface. The external diameter of the bone increases, and the wall becomes thinner. Haversian canals enlarge, and the space that develops in the bone becomes filled with adipose and fibrous tissue. The thinning of the cortex of the long bones weakens them, and fractures occur under even slight loads.

The loss of bone mass is unequal between the sexes. At age 20 years, bone mass is greater in women than in men. The bone loss that begins in young adulthood is more rapid in women, so that by age 50 years, bone mass is equal in the two sexes. After menopause, bone loss accelerates in women and the incidence of osteoporosis is several times higher than in men. A woman aged 80 years has one chance in five of sustaining a fracture of the neck of the femur.

Many factors are involved in this process of mineral depletion, and the following explanations have been offered:

1. After growth and modeling of bone are completed in the young adult, an imbalance of osteoclastic and osteoblastic activity develops. This imbalance is exacerbated by the sudden withdrawal of estrogen during the menopause.

2. Calcitonin secretion is modified by the level of circulating estrogen. As estrogen levels fall, the balance between parathormone and calcitonin shifts in favor of parathormone, which affects bone directly and increases the renal excretion of minerals.

3. There is an age-related decrease in the circulating level of hydroxylated vitamin D_3, which impairs intestinal absorption of calcium and causes an increasing reliance on bone for the maintenance of adequate calcium levels.

Significant bone mineral loss occurs from the vertebrae in both sexes but more markedly in the postmenopausal female. Spinal curvatures increase, giving rise to the so-called "dowager's hump." Shortening of the cervical vertebrae can also lead to kinking of the vertebral arteries, a contributing factor in some of the temporary ischemic attacks experienced by old people.

MUSCLE

Characteristic of the aging process is a loss of muscle mass. Studies on cadavers have shown a loss of about 30% in total muscle mass between the third and eighth decade. The loss is very nonuniform; red muscle is lost to a greater extent than white, and loss in individual muscles is inversely related to the extent to which they continue to be active during aging. Muscle cells show the general signs of cellular aging, the accumulation of lipofuscin, and an increase in lipid content. The loss of muscle mass involves a reduction in both the number and size of muscle fibers. Sarcomeres are lost from the fibers, thereby reducing the effective length. As with most aging tissues, there is an increase in extracellular components, specifically an increase in connective tissue. The reduction in active fiber length and the increase in fibrous tissue limit the tension that can be developed at any muscle length and reduce the effective range of motion. Exercise of the muscle can, however, minimize these functional changes.

In the senescent experimental animal, it has been shown that the loss of muscle mass correlates well with the decrease in number of myofibrils. Changes can be seen in the sarcolemma, and the T-tubule system proliferates. In the periphery of the muscle fiber, there is evidence of continued protein synthesis, but the product does not become organized into contractile elements. Presumably, this represents abortive attempts at regeneration. Muscle spindles become reduced in diameter, but there appears to be no reduction in number.

At the motor end plate, an unfolding of the membrane and a reduction of the area occupied by the junction occur. The aging muscle shows an absolute fall in the content of ATP, a decrease in the ATP/ADP ratio, and a fall in the content of both glycogen and creatine phosphate.

There is no change in the resting membrane potential of aging muscle, but there is a reduction in the frequency of miniature end-plate potentials—i.e., a reduction in the spontaneous release of quanta of neurotransmitter. This may reflect reduced synthesis and axonal transport in the motor nerves. In the old individual, the electromyogram typically shows a decrease in amplitude, a prolongation of the individual action potentials, and an increase in the number of polyphasic potentials. There is also evidence of an increase in both absolute and relative refractory periods in senescent muscle. The latent period, contraction period, and relaxation period are lengthened, and the rate of development of peak tension is reduced.

Changes in the overall muscle strength begin at approximately age 35 years, but the degree of loss differs widely among muscle groups. Moreover, the assessment of muscle strength in the old individual is likely to be confused by changes in motivation, joint stiffness, and the ability of the muscle to obtain adequate oxygenation.

There is an age-related loss of motoneurons, but their number is reduced less than that of muscle fibers. As a consequence, the size of the motor units is reduced. For a muscle to work against a particular load, therefore, an increased number of motor units must be recruited, and the person perceives this as an increase in effort.

SKIN AND APPENDAGES

Skin serves a number of vital functions. It is a major receptor site for collecting information at the interface between the body and the environment; it is a rather impermeable barrier preventing loss of water from the body; it is a barrier against invasion by microorganisms; and by virtue of its high vascularity, it acts as the major organ of thermoregulation.

Unlike other organs, the skin, in some areas at least, is exposed to the potentially harmful wavelengths of light. This radiation affects all the cellular elements of the skin, and the changes produced, the condition of dermatoheliosis, are difficult to separate from the true aging changes.

The epidermis consists of a stratified epithelium containing a basal germinal layer of cuboidal cells superimposed on which are the keratinocytes, which, as they migrate toward the surface, undergo a series of changes to ultimately become the anuclear, fully differentiated "cells" that are shed. The renewal time of the skin is estimated to be about 2 months. The epidermis also contains two cell types that arise elsewhere and migrate to the epidermis. These are the melanocytes, which derive from the neural crest and comprise about 5% of the epidermal cells, and the Langerhans cells, which are formed in the bone marrow and, in the skin, form the reticuloepithelial system. These cells form a part of the immune system, and they are identified by the presence of cell-surface Ia antigens.

The epidermis and its basement membrane invaginates into the corium to form an undulant surface, the rete ridges or pegs. As the skin ages, the number of germinal cells diminishes and the rete ridges become smoothed out. The mechanical strength of the junction between epidermis and corium is reduced, and this may account for the greater ease with which old skin blisters. Melanocytes diminish in number as do the Langerhans cells. Chronic sun exposure serves to increase the number of melanocytes but contributes to the loss of Langerhans cells. The reduction in density of melanocytes produces the "aging pallor." The corium, or dermis, which lies between the epidermal basement membrane and the subcutaneous fat contains the connective tissue, blood vessels, nerves, receptors, and the sweat glands and the pilosebaceous units. The connective tissue is comprised of ground substance, collagen, and elastic fibers. The collagen is arranged in a spiral form and, in association with the elastin, serves to hold the skin tightly bunched and attached to the underlying tissue. As it ages, the ground substance tends to become dehydrated and the fibrous elements lose their elastic properties so that in the old, the skin appears thin and falls into wrinkles and folds. Wrinkling affects the whole body surface but is especially obvious in heavy use areas such as those overlying the muscles of facial expression. Aging changes in the density of fibroblasts contribute to delayed wound healing.

Hair growth and pigmentation and sebum production are independent activities. Both are affected by aging. A reduced activity of melanocytes is responsible for graying of the hair. This is reliably age-related in the axillary and pubic sites but less reliably so for scalp hair where graying appears to be more genetically determined. Graying begins at about 30 years of age in whites and somewhat later in blacks. Hair loss occurs in both sexes with an onset around 30 years in males, and in females, after menopause. Axillary and pubic hair are lost at a rate less than that of scalp hair; the pattern is one of loss from the periphery inwards. Loss of the outer third of the eyebrows, which is a common sign of myxedema, occurs in many older individuals. Old men may show an increased growth of hair in the nostrils and around the borders of the ears.

Sebum production falls after age 60 years in the female and around 70 years in the male, although the glands may show an increase in size. Both apocrine and ecrine sweat glands are reduced in number except for the ecrine glands of the scalp. Reduced secretory rates occur in both types of gland, but the cause may reside outside of the secretory structure, i.e., the glands may respond to neurotransmitters less effectively.

The cutaneous nerves do not appear to be changed significantly by age so that the complement of free nerve endings is unaltered. Meissner's corpuscles and the pacinian corpuscles are reduced, and surviving receptors become irregular in shape.

Nail growth slows with aging, and changes in nail composition, mainly calcium deposition, result in a dull, yellow appearance. The half-moon, the lunula, disappears, and longitudinal ridging develops. Thickening of the nails is much more marked on the toes than the fingers, and toenails become hooked and curved.

Loss of subcutaneous adipose tissue in many parts of the body, especially the limbs, reduces the skin's effectiveness as a thermal insulator. Defense against entry of microorganisms is impaired both by drying out of the superficial layers and by reduction in the number of the Langerhan's cells. Age does not appear to impair the skin's role as a barrier to the loss of water vapor.

TEETH AND ORAL STRUCTURES

The state of the teeth at any particular time is more the result of dental hygiene than of aging. Although substantial numbers of people over the age of 65 years have either no natural teeth at all or none in one or the other jaw, the situation has vastly improved over the past 10 years as a result of fluoridation of water supplies reducing the incidence of caries and improved hygiene slowing the occurrence of periodontal disease. Loss of teeth is more common in the maxilla than in the mandible. Although the teeth are exposed to constant abrasion, they are so durable that it has been suggested that under ideal conditions, they should last for at least two life spans. Healthy, well-preserved teeth do, however, show some true signs of aging.

The major change observed in *enamel* is loss through attrition and the development of pigmentation in the superficial layers. Animal experiments have suggested that associated with the increased pigmentation is a decrease in the permeability (already very small) of the enamel. *Dentin* is a dynamic component of the teeth, and its formation is stimulated by a number of factors, including wear, caries, and irritation. The dentin is also believed to be laid down as a normal aging process. There appears to be a cycling between odontoblasts and cells of the dental pulp, with odontoblasts degenerating or differentiating into pulp cells and cells from the pulp replacing the lost cells. The continued odontoblastic activity reduces the size of the pulp cavity. With aging, the dentin becomes more opaque and less hydrated and has an increased fluoride content.

Dental pulp diminishes in volume as its space is invaded by dentin, and by age 70 years, the pulp space of many teeth has been obliterated. The cell population of the pulp, mainly fibroblasts, decreases beginning in the early twenties. Age-related changes are also seen in the blood vessels and the nerve supply of the pulp, so there is a progressive reduction of both perfusion and sensitivity. The connective tissue of the pulp, which consists of ground substance, reticular fibers, and collagen, becomes more dense with dehydration of the ground substance and fibrosis. With the increasing density of fibers in the pulp areas of calcification, "pulpstones" appear.

The cement substance that invests the root of the tooth continues to be laid down throughout life. Although the rate of formation diminishes, the tooth is still attached to the periodontal tissues. The periodontal ligament, which serves as a suspensory sling for the tooth, is attached to the cement substance and the alveolar bone. With aging, the ligament is thinned and the fibers lose their alignment. This is probably the result of a reduction of the load placed on the ligament as occlusal teeth are lost or a diet requiring less mastication is adopted and is not a real aging effect.

The gingiva or gum consists of two parts: the attached gingiva, which covers the alveolar bone, and the free gingiva, which forms a cuff around the enamel of the tooth. Since the free part of the gum is not attached, there is a potential space or cleft. The common change of aging is the recession of the gum away from the tooth, thus exposing the junction between enamel and cement substances and forming a pocket in which bacteria and food debris can lodge. The stratified epithelium of the gum thins and loses the degree of keratinization that is present in the young.

The alveolar bone participates in the general loss of bone mineral with age, and the bone matrix is resorbed. This process of resorption accelerates when teeth are lost.

The epithelial lining of the mouth undergoes a slowing of cell proliferation, and the healing of abrasions is impaired. In addition, the surface becomes drier as a result of reduced mucin secretion coupled with a reduced flow from the salivary glands. The epithelial surface of the tongue becomes smooth as filiform papillae are lost. In the circumvallate papillae, taste buds atrophy and produce changes in the gustatory sensation. A person aged 70 years has only 30% of the original complement of taste buds.

Prosthetic replacement of teeth reduces taste sensation and fails to restore normal masticatory ability. In addition, a prothesis robs the individual of texture sense, which contributes to the enjoyment of food. These factors influence a person's food selection. There is a tendency for the older person to choose salty or very sweet foods that require little chewing.

SUGGESTED READING

Blood

Bowdler AJ, Dougherty RM, Bowdler NC: Age as a factor affecting erythrocyte osmotic fragility in males. *Gerontology* 1981; 27:224–231.

Cerny LC, Cook LB, Valone F: The erythrocyte in aging. *Exp Gerontol* 1972; 7:137–142.

Goldman R: Decline in organ function with aging, in Rossman I (ed): *Clinical Geriatrics*. Philadelphia, JB Lippincott Co, 1979, p 42.

Hyams DE: The blood, in Brocklehurst JC (ed): *Textbook of Geriatric Medicine and Gastroenterology*. New York, Churchill Livingstone, Inc, 1973, p 528–532.

Supporting Tissues

Beausoleil N, Sparrow D, Rowe J, et al: Longitudinal analysis of the influence of age on bone loss in men. *Gerontologist* 1980; 20:63.

Ciara SM: Bone loss and aging, in Goldman R, Rockstein M (eds): *The Physiology and Pathology of Aging*. New York, Academic Press, 1975.

Exton-Smith AN: Bone aging and metabolic bone disease, in Brocklehurst JC (ed): *Textbook of Geriatric Medicine and Gerontology*, New York, Churchill Livingston, Inc, 1973, p 476–491.

Gordon GS, Genant HK: The aging skeleton. *Clin Geriatr Med* 1985; 1:95–118.

Hall DA: Metabolic and structural aspects of aging, in Brocklehurst JC (ed): *Textbook of Geriatric Medicine and Gerontology*. New York, Churchill Livingston, Inc, 1973, p 21–32.

Muscle

Gutman E: Muscle, in Finch EC, Hayflick L (eds): *Handbook of the Biology of Aging*. New York, Van Nostrand Reinhold Co, 1977.

Shephard RJ: *Endurance Fitness*. Toronto, University of Toronto Press, 1977.

Shephard RJ: *Physical Activity and Aging*. New York, Croom Helm, 1978.

Shock NW, Norris AH: Neuromuscular coordination as a factor in age changes in muscular exercise, in Brumer D, Jokl E (eds): *Physical Activity and Aging*. Baltimore, University Park Press, 1970.

Skin

Gomez EC, Berman B: The aging skin. *Clin Geriatr Med* 1985; 1:285–305.

Oral Cavity
Zack L: The oral cavity, in Rossman I (ed): *Clinical Geriatrics*. Philadelphia, JB Lippincott, Co, 1979, p 618–637.

5

The Respiratory and Cardiovascular Systems

Many people first appreciate the process of aging when they realize that everyday tasks require more effort than before and that they can sustain decreasing levels of physical activity. This decline is early in its onset and insidious in its progress. A healthy 30-year-old, for example, would be hard pressed to match the sustained activity of a 10-year-old at play. Changes in the muscle and the supporting tissues contribute to this functional decline, but a major role is played by the person's decreased ability to acquire and deliver oxygen to the active tissues. Each step in the path oxygen takes from the air to the metabolizing cell is vulnerable to aging.

RESPIRATORY SYSTEM

During the course of a lifetime, a typical person will ventilate about 3×10^5 m³ of atmospheric air—air that, in addition to a variety of aerosols and particulate matter, may contain as much as 1% of organic and inorganic contaminants. As with other systems, it is difficult to decide how much the changes seen, over the course of years, represent aging and how much environmental damage. Some studies of the aging lung have tried to use a population in which such hazards as city dwelling, a hostile work environment, and the elective pollution of smoking are avoided. More often, studies are based on more typical life experiences that include such hazards.

Full development of the respiratory system in terms of airways, gas exchange areas, and vasculature is achieved in the early 20s but functional maturation, in terms of dynamic gas exchange, continues into the 40s. In large part, this comes about by an increase in power of the respiratory muscles and an improved disposition of the thorax as posture becomes more erect.

As the lung ages, the fraction of lung volume occupied by airways increases at the expense of alveolar space. The trachea and the major airways increase in diameter and become stiffer as the cartilage calcifies; more volume is taken up by respiratory bronchioles and alveolar ducts. At maturity, the lungs contain about 3×10^8 alveoli, which provide an alveolar exchange surface of approximately 80 m². While the number of alveoli remains virtually constant in the healthy aging lung, the alveoli become smaller and more shallow, thus reducing the alveolar surface area to 65 to 70 m² at 70 years of age.

The lung loses elasticity as it ages, but this is not attributable to loss of elastin, which is reported as increasing in amount. Rather, it appears to be due to changes in the collagen, which has a helical arrangement around alveoli and alveolar ducts. This spring-like arrangement makes a major contribution to the recoil properties. The collagen stiffens and forms cross-linkages, thus interfering with the elasticity of the helices. A further contribution to lung elasticity arises from surface forces at the air-alveolar interface. The extent to which pulmonary surfactant is altered by age is presently unknown. In the experimental animal, there is a reduction in the number of surfactant-producing alveolar type II cells. The compliance of the lung increases (Fig 5–1), and a lesser inward-directed force is exerted on the chest wall. As a result, the position at rest of the thorax, determined by the balance of inward pull of the lungs and outward pull of the chest wall, occurs at a higher lung volume than in the young.

Changes in the thorax involving calcification and consequent stiffening of cartilaginous articulations of the ribs, together with increases in the spinal curvatures, make the chest wall less compliant. This reduction in compliance outweighs the increased compliance of the lung; thus, the overall compliance of the system decreases (see Fig 5–1).

More muscular work is required, therefore, to move air in and out of the lung. The diaphragm contributes significantly to changes in the thoracic volume, and this is exploited to an increased extent in older persons to minimize the extra effort involved in expanding the stiffened rib cage. This increased reliance on the diaphragm makes the ventilation of the older person especially sensitive to changes in intra-abdominal pressure, whether caused by a large meal or by body position.

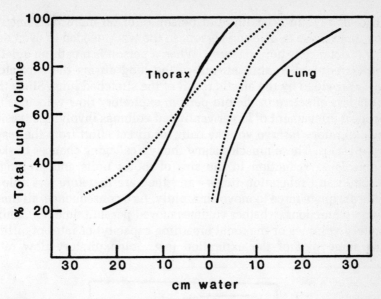

FIG 5–1.
The changing compliance of the lung and thoracic wall. *Solid lines* represent the 25-year-old; *dotted lines* the 70-year-old. (Based on data from Turner JM, Mead J, Wohl MEJ: Elasticity of human lungs in relation to age. *Appl Physiol* 1968; 25:664–671.)

The thoracic musculature is generally well maintained, and the diaphragm shows no loss of mass with aging. However, the muscles share with muscle in general the increased duration of both contraction and relaxation phases. In some old people, the contractile forces of the muscles may be sufficient to distort ribs weakened by demineralization so that the chest becomes pinched, to the detriment of thoracic volumes.

There is a tendency for pulmonary vascular resistance to increase perhaps due to a reduction in the elastic stretch that is supplied by the parenchyma. The vasoconstrictor response to alveolar hypoxia is blunted with age, but there appears to be no change in distribution of perfusion within the lung at resting volumes.

Figure 5–2 illustrates the age-related changes in lung volumes. The change in total lung capacity is small; the major changes are in the residual volume and expiratory reserve volume, both of which can be explained by the reduced compliance of the thorax. Functional residual capacity increases; inspiratory capacity and vital capacity are reduced. Figure 5–2 suggests that tidal volume increases with age, and this is in keeping with the fact that anatomical dead space volume increases due to enlargement of the airways. Alveolar ventilation remains relatively constant, and there appears to be no consistent change in ventilatory pattern.

The airways in a healthy old person offer no more resistance to airflow than those in a young person, so the work needed to overcome airway resistance is not increased. When a person is breathing quietly, the work required to shift air out of the lung during the expiratory phase is provided by the elastic recoil of the stretched lung. Since this recoil is less effective in the old person, expiratory flow velocities are reduced. Achievement of larger ventilated volumes involving invasion of the expiratory reserve volume calls for direct effort from the respiratory muscles. These muscles show the typical aging changes of skeletal muscle—a reduction in the size of motor units and prolonged contraction and relaxation times—and they are therefore less able to provide adequate force to move air rapidly. As a consequence, all timed ventilatory functions, whether volumes moved per unit time (e.g., forced expiratory volumes or maximal breathing capacity) or rates of airflow during some part of the expiration (e.g., midexpiratory flow rate),

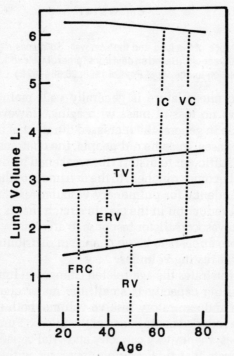

FIG 5–2.
Age-related changes in lung volume. The values are appropriate for a man 180 cm tall. (*VC* = vital capacity; *IC* = inspiratory capacity; *TV* = tidal volume; *ERV* = expiratory reserve volume; *FRC* = functional residual capacity; and *RV* = residual volume.)

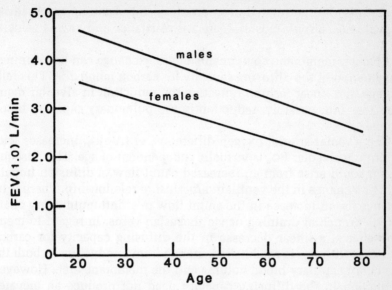

FIG 5–3.
Age-related change in forced expiratory volume (1 second) in men and women. FEV$_{(1.0)}$ is highly dependent on stature. The values given are for a man 180 cm tall and a woman 165 cm tall. (Based on data from Berglund E, Birath G, Burke J, et al: Spirometric studies of normal subjects. *Acta Med Scand* 1963; 173:185–206.)

decrease significantly in the aged person who is free of lung disease (Fig 5–3).

The elasticity of the lung parenchyma maintains the patency of the small airways. At some point in an active expiration, pressures sufficient to close the small airways develop. The volume of air in the lung at this time is called the "closing volume." This closure phenomenon affects the basal parts of the lung to a greater extent than the more apical parts, since the latter are more stretched by the dependent weight of the lung. Consequently, the later fractions of a forced expiration to residual volume are derived entirely from the apical areas, which by virtue of their larger resting size, receive little of the preceding inspiration. The closing volume in a young person is greater than the residual volume, but it is still much less than the functional residual capacity. In the older person, the closing volume increases and may equal or even exceed the functional residual capacity. Consequently, some parts of the lung are unventilated for major periods of the breathing cycle.

This closure effect is seen in the expiratory flow/volume curve in which velocity of expiratory flow is plotted as a function of lung volume. At high lung volumes, there is no age-related impairment of flow velocity despite the reduction in elastic recoil of the lungs. At lower lung volumes, airway closure increases resistance and lowers velocity (Fig 5–4).

Alveolar membrane components of gas exchange can be examined by evaluation of the diffusing capacity for carbon monoxide. This falls with age in a linear fashion reflecting the reduction in alveolar membrane area and, possibly, reduction in the pulmonary capillary blood volume.

The alveolar-arterial oxygen difference, or $(A-a)O_2$, increases with age, but the alveolar PO_2 is virtually independent of age. This disequilibrium could arise from an increased shunt flow, a diffusion impairment, or a change in the ventilation/perfusion relationship. There is no evidence for an increase in the shunt flow over intrapulmonary channels via bronchial draining or via thebesian veins. In regard to membrane effects, a linear decrease in the diffusing capacity for carbon monoxide with age is established, arising from a reduction in both the pulmonary capillary blood volume and the membrane area. However, a reduction in the diffusing capacity need not produce an elevated $(A-a)O_2$. That the phenomenon may be attributable in part to the uneven ventilation resulting from closure is supported by the observation that disequilibrium is less at large ventilated volumes when airways that

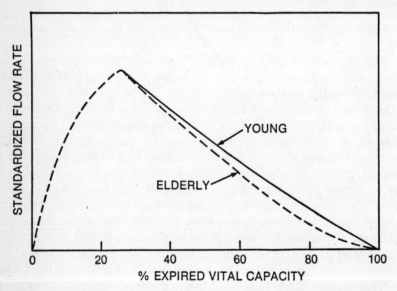

FIG 5–4.
The age-related shift in the flow velocity/volume curve. Flow velocity is standardized to total lung capacity.

would otherwise be closed are open and ventilation/perfusion uniformity is more nearly achieved.

In the lungs of older persons, the defense against inhaled particulate matter is reduced. Cilia are lost from the airways, and the vigor of the remaining cilia is reduced. The "mucus escalator" thus becomes less effective in removing material from the peripheral lung. The macrophages that form the final line of defense at the alveolar level also become less efficient. The consequence for the old person chronically exposed to particle-laden air is an additional decrease in oxygen uptake by occlusion of more than the already reduced alveolar surface. Although the hemoglobin concentration is maintained within normal limits in the healthy elderly person, there is a small alteration in red blood cell metabolism, which produces a decreased concentration of 2,3-diphosphoglycerate (DPG). As a consequence, the oxygen dissociation curve is shifted to the left, thus making the unloading of oxygen in the tissues more difficult.

Evidence points to a blunting of the ventilatory response to hypoxemia and hypercapnia, and this has been related to a reduced outflow from respiratory motor neurons, although alterations in the sensitivity of the chemoreceptors, both central and peripheral, provide an alternative explanation. In exercise, however, ventilatory response is greater in the old than the young despite the blunted chemical regulation. This extra ventilated volume will compensate for the older person's increased dead space so that isocapnic conditions can be maintained.

CARDIOVASCULAR SYSTEM

The heart and blood vessels are highly dependent for their normal function on the physical properties of distensibility, contractility, and elasticity, all of which involve connective tissue as well as muscle. Heart weight, expressed as a fraction of body weight, tends to increase slightly, although the capacity for stress-induced hypertrophy is reduced in older hearts. Evidence of some degree of age-related left ventricular hypertrophy has been obtained by direct measurement in the rat and by echocardiographic studies in man. With aging, there is an increase, primarily in the immediate epicardial and endocardial regions rather than generally throughout the chamber walls, in the ratio of collagen to muscle in the myocardium. However, the myocardium has a general increased stiffness rather than stiffness localized to these regions, and it has been suggested that the significant change is in the character of the connective tissue matrix rather than simply in the amount. The myocardial cells are a favored site for the deposition of the aging pigment lipofuscin, and the fraction of myocardial volume occupied by pigment increases linearly with age. However, how much of this accumulation is age dependent is open to question since increases in myocardial lipofuscin are also seen in chronic diseases and in malnutrition. The mitochondria increase in number and decrease in size. The valves of the heart occasionally show an increase in fibrous tissue and signs of calcium deposition.

A major structural alteration of the arteries is an increase in collagen and smooth muscle with some reduction in elastic tissue. As elsewhere in the body, the collagen tends to become cross-linked, and calcium is deposited in the framework so generated. The intima thickens and is invaded by modified smooth muscle cells, which synthesize connective tissue proteins. The arteries show reduced compliance with age; the volume change produced by a pressure increase of 100 mm Hg at age 60 years is only half of that in vessels of the 20-year-old person. This loss of compliance represents a serious reduction in the capacity of the aorta to store part of the stroke volume, but it is compensated to some extent by an increase in aortic size. This expansion does not continue after age 60 years, however, with the consequence that the load on the left ventricle increases. The increase in arterial stiffness also leads to both an increase in the velocity of pulse-wave transmission (which doubles between ages 20 and 60 years) and a decrease in the amplification of the arterial pulse between the aorta and the femoral artery. Veins become increasingly tortuous with age; the intima thickens, and there is progressive fibrosis of the tunica media. The loss of elastic tissue weakens the vessel wall, and the varicosities occur in veins subjected to high pressure. Capillaries show a thickening of the basement membrane; fenestrations of the endothelium become fewer. These changes, taken in association with the increasing density of ground substance of the connective tissues, threaten adequate diffusional nutrition of the parenchyma.

The functional characteristics of the aging myocardium have been studied in isolated muscle preparations taken from experimental animals. Resting tension shows a greater rise with increasing length than it does in younger muscle, but there is no difference in the maximum isometric tension or the muscle length at which that tension is achieved. Both the time to peak isometric tension and the duration of the relaxation phase are prolonged: this is consistent with a reduced ability of the sarcoplasmic reticulum to sequester calcium or some alteration in the dynamics of an anatomically unidentified calcium storage pool.

The plateau phase of the myocardial action potential is prolonged; this too could involve an alteration in calcium movement. The myocyte, as it ages, displays a lowered responsiveness to β-adrenergic stimulation, and biochemical analysis of this change demonstrates that the defect lies distal to both the membrane receptor and the protein kinase system.

The sinoatrial (SA) node shows a loss of cells beginning in the young adult and accelerating after the age of 60 years. The node becomes invaded by fibrous tissue, and in the very old heart, as few as 10% of the original cell population remains. Even so, the pacemaker function of the node is largely unimpaired. Cell loss is also seen in the atrioventricular (AV) node, the His bundle, and in the bundle branches. Loss of cells is seen earlier in the bundle than in the AV node which may remain unaffected until the age of 70 years.

Some information about the contractile state of the human myocardium can be obtained noninvasively by measurement of the so-called systolic time intervals. The time relationships of the systolic events of the cardiac cycle can be studied by the simultaneous recording of the electrocardiogram (ECG), the heart sounds, and the contour of the carotid pulse. The systolic time intervals so obtained are (1) the period of electromechanical systole (EMS) measured from the Q wave of the ECG to the start of the high-frequency component of the second heart sound and (2) the left ventricular ejection time (LVET) measured from the start of the rapid upstroke of the carotid pulse contour to the dicrotic notch. The difference between these intervals is the pre-ejection period (PEP)—i.e., $PEP = EMS - LVET$.

Both EMS and LVET change inversely in a closely linear fashion with changes in the heart rate, so they are usually expressed as indices. For example, LVET index = $LVET + a \times HR$, where a is the slope of the regression of LVET on heart rate and HR is heart rate. Left ventricular ejection time or an index shows little change with age, but the PEP lengthens on the order of 15% between ages 25 and 65 years. As a consequence, EMS lengthens slightly over this age span. Lengthening of the PEP can result from a reduced inotropic state of the myocardium (a reduced resting sympathetic tonus), a reduced end-diastolic volume, or an alteration in the contractile properties themselves. It is likely that all three contribute, with the myocardial effect being the greatest. It is known that aged myofibrils have reduced activity of adenosine triphosphatase, in conjunction with changes in the intracardiac connective tissue. This may be basic to the extended contraction time of isolated cardiac muscle referred to earlier. The PEP also contains the time elements of excitation of the myocardium and excitation-contraction coupling. Although there is no evidence of reduced dromotropy (velocity

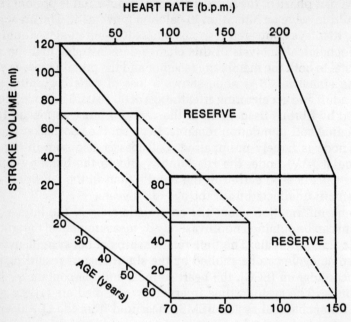

FIG 5–5.
The change in resting cardiac output and reserve of output between young adulthood and 70 years of age. Cardiac output equals the area defined by stroke volume × heart rate. b.p.m. = beats per minute. (From Kenney RA: Physiology of Aging. *Clin Geriatr Med* 1985; 1:37–59. Used by permission.)

of conduction of excitation) with age in the healthy heart, changes in the transverse tubule system of the cardiac muscle fibers could well modify the coupling time.

When a person is between age 20 and 80 years, cardiac output decreases approximately 1% per year, while the stroke volume decreases 0.7% per year. These observations taken together imply a reduction in the resting heart rate, although direct investigation of the relationship of heart rate and age give no clear evidence of an increase or a decrease. The maximum heart rate that can be achieved, however, does change in a linear fashion with age and may be predicted from the following relationship:

$$\text{Maximum HR} = 220 - \text{age in years}$$

This reduction in chronotropic response may be the result of a change in the number of β-adrenergic receptors in the heart, a reduced release of neurotransmitters or changes in the sinoatrial pacemaker cells as a result of the invasion of the mode by fibrous tissues (Fig 5–5).

Bradycardia induced by breath holding in the end quiet expiratory position or by immersion of the face in water is significantly less marked in the old than in the young. This reaction is less in old persons who are in good physical condition (particularly swimmers), and in fact, the "aging" change can be seen in sedentary, unconditioned young people. This changed responsiveness is interpreted as indicating a less effective vagal recruitment in the old or, again, a reduced responsiveness of the old sinoatrial node. Systolic time intervals recorded under these circumstances demonstrate that withdrawal of sympathetic stimulation occurs more slowly and to a lesser extent in the old. Following combined cholinergic and sympathetic blockade, the heart rate is slower in old than in young subjects. This indicates a reduced inherent sinus rhythm. The aged heart shows a reduced response of tachycardia to tilting, stemming probably from reduced baroreceptor sensitivity as a consequence of stiffening of the arterial wall.

Heart work tends to decrease slightly with age, while the total peripheral resistance increases steadily at a rate of approximately 1% per year from age 40 years onward. The tendency, therefore, is for perfusion to be decreased. The extent of decreased perfusion is variable among organs; it is dramatic in the kidney (50%) as well as in the splanchnic and cutaneous circulations. Cerebral blood flow (measured in milliliters of blood/minute/100 g of tissue) decreases by about 20% over 40 years. Changes in the resting flow to the myocardium and skeletal muscle are less marked. However, the reaction of hyperemia following tissue hypoxia is significantly less in the old than in the young.

Under circumstances of physical activity, the impedance of the vasculature is more significant than the conventionally calculated resistance. Arterial impedance is dependent on several factors including heart rate, vascular compliance, and viscosity of the blood. Under the low output conditions of rest, the impedance factor is relatively minor, but in the older subject, reduced arterial compliance combined with the elevated output of exercise makes impedance a major element of the loading of the myocardium and thus a factor in increasing the dimensions of the left ventricle.

Many of the factors already discussed would be expected to increase arterial pressure, although the increase in aortic volume and the decrease in stroke volume would operate in the opposite direction. Longitudinal and cross-sectional studies have shown an increase in the systolic pressure with age, with a lesser rate of increase in the diastolic pressure. In the very old, diastolic pressure may fall. The rate at which the pressure rises correlates with blood pressure in the earlier years of life; the higher the initial pressure, the more rapid the rise. There are major questions, however, whether this increase in blood pressure is an inevitable consequence of healthy aging. Individuals who live in isolated, primitive societies do not show an increase in pressure as they age, nor do chronic psychiatric patients who grow old in a protected institutional environment. It may well be that the age-related rise in pressure is more a consequence of environmental factors, including diet and social stresses. Physical conditioning can slow or even reverse the rise; in some individuals, relaxation techniques reinforced by bio-feedback are effective. Older persons fail to maintain the arterial pressure on tilting as might be expected in view of the diminished baroreceptor sensitivity, but there is no apparent effect of age on the rise of arterial pressure during exercise. Typical of the aging individual is sluggishness of the return of both heart rate and blood pressure to resting levels following perturbation.

A major design objective of the respiratory and cardiovascular systems is the appropriate delivery of atmospheric oxygen to the active cells, and together they form the oxygen conductance system. Table 5–1 lists the sequence of processes in the chain of conductance and the functional factors involved. Examination of this list of factors reveals the vulnerability of oxygen conductance to impairment by aging. The implications are considered in the next section.

PHYSICAL ACTIVITY AND AGING

The age-related changes in the cardiovascular and respiratory systems that operate to impair the conductance of oxygen from the atmosphere to the active cells have been considered. Minor changes at each step in the pathway add up to produce a rather linear fall in the maximum Vo_2 that can be achieved (Fig 5–6). It is important to note that this aging decline in physical capacity can be reproduced in a healthy young person by a period of enforced bed rest. Under these circumstances, cardiac output decreases, ventilatory capacity falls, lean body mass is lost, adipose tissue is gained, and mineral is lost from bone. Three weeks of bed rest can simulate the changes that regularly occur over the span of 25 years. Clearly, these aging changes are as much the product of reduced activity as its cause. It is therefore necessary to recognize that the aging decline in function may involve three factors: (1) a genuine physiologic aging change, (2) the manifestation of "hypokinetic disease" described above, and (3) some early, undiagnosed pathology of the oxygen conductance system.

If instead of examining the limit of oxygen consumption, we concern ourselves with the customary level of daily activity, a different relationship to age is seen (Fig 5–7). The number of calories expended declines steadily from childhood onward. This decline affects both the basal rate of energy expenditure, which, as we have already seen, reflects a changing lean body mass and the expenditure of activity calories. Typically, caloric expenditure in physical activity shows two major accelerations in the slope of decline. The first is likely to occur in the forties when there is a tendency in many people to give up the more energetic leisure time pursuits—one of the manifestations of "so-

TABLE 5–1.
The Oxygen Conductance System*

Process	Factors Involved
Ventilation: ability to maintain a supply of air to the alveoli	Thoracic compliance[t] Lung compliance[t] Airway resistance[t] Vital capacity[t] Timed ventilatory function, e.g., maximal voluntary ventilation (MVV)[t] Closing volume[t] Chemoreceptor drive to ventilation[t]
Diffusion: movement of gas from the terminal bronchioles, where bulk flow ceases, into the alveolar sacs; the movement of gases across the alveolar membrane	Length of terminal airways[t] Size of the alveolar sac[t] Area of the alveolar membrane[t] Thickness of the membrane Alveolar PO_2
Uptake: uptake of the available oxygen by blood flowing in the pulmonary capillaries	Pulmonary perfusion rate[t] Shunting of blood[t] Ventilation/perfusion ratio[t] Hemoglobin concentration Association characteristics of hemoglobin
Delivery: distribution of the available oxygen to the tissues	Tissue perfusion rate[t] Dissociation characteristics of hemoglobin[t] Tissue PO_2
Diffusion: movement of the oxygen from the tissue capillary to the active cell	Capillary density, i.e., proximity to cell[t] Nature of the interstitium[t] Pressure gradient for oxygen Myoglobin concentration
Utilization: metabolism of oxygen by the cell	Intracellular enzyme systems[t] Intracellular environment[t]

*From Kenney RA: Physiology of aging, *Clin Geriatr Med* 1985; 1:37–59. Used by permission.
[t]Changed by aging.

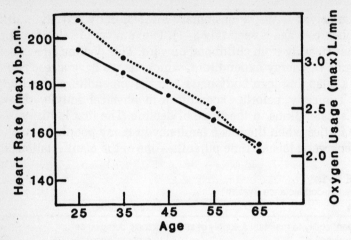

FIG 5–6.
The similar course of the decrease in maximum heart rate (*solid line*) and maximum oxygen consumption (*dotted line*) in aging men. b.p.m. = beats per minute. (Based on Astrand I, Astrand P: Aerobic work performance: A review, in Folinsbee LJ, et al. (eds): *Environmental Stress,* New York, Academic Press, 1978, pp 149–163.)

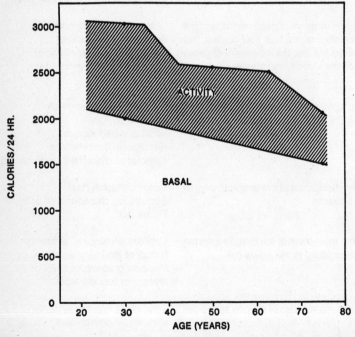

FIG 5–7.
The fall in energy expenditure with age—both basal expenditure and that attributable to activity. (From Kenney RA: Physiology of aging. *Clin Geriatr Med* 1985; 1:37–59. Used by permission.)

ciogenic aging" defined by Alex Comfort. The second tends to occur with retirement from employment.

A convenient means of evaluating an individual's activity level is by means of the MET scale. The MET is a unit of metabolism, and a single MET is that level of activity involved in sitting quietly in a comfortable environment. A value of 1 MET equates with 50 calories/m²/hour or an oxygen consumption of 3.5 ml/kg of body weight per minute. Table 5–2 lists MET values for some typical daily activities. Using these values, one can construct an energy diary for 24 hours in a person's life. This can then be used descriptively or prescriptively in balancing activity and caloric intake, for example. This scale also provides a convenient way of assessing the adequacy of a person's oxygen conductance system by observing the levels of activity of which they are capable. For example, a person who can climb a flight of stairs without becoming breathless is capable of an oxygen consumption of better than 20 ml/kg/minute. Some caution is necessary in using these values in older individuals with mobility problems since these may make some activities unusually "oxygen-expensive." An alternative evaluation of cardiorespiratory condition is provided by measurement of heart rate at a particular MET level and of the speed with which it returns to normal.

TABLE 5–2.
Metabolic Cost of Various Activities

Activity	MET
Sleeping	0.8
Sitting at rest	1.0
Secretarial work	1.5–2.0
Light housework	2.5
Scrubbing, polishing	3.0–4.0
Driving a car	1.5–2.5
Walking, 3 mph	3.0
Carrying a 10 kg load	4.0
Climbing stairs	6.0
Mowing lawn (hand mower)	4.0–6.0
Mowing lawn (power mower)	2.5–3.5
Light carpentry	6.0
Painting (house)	4.0–5.0
Bowling	2.0–4.0
Tennis (doubles)	5.0
Jogging	7.0
Golf (walking)	5.0
Golf (cart)	3.0
Conditioning exercises	3.0–8.0

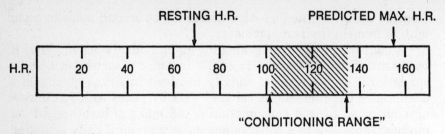

FIG 5–8.
The use of heart-rate interval in establishing the conditioning zone for elderly persons.

Before the reality of hypokinetic disease was established, it was generally contended that little if any improvement of physical capacity could be expected from conditioning programs for older people. However, it is apparent that, in fact, older persons are as trainable as younger ones in attaining a given percentage change over the preconditioning status. Conditioning programs for older persons must recognize the lessened flexibility available in the cardiorespiratory system. The maximum heart rate, for example, diminishes with age thus limiting the range over which it may respond. A useful concept in this connection is the "heart-rate interval," the difference between the resting heart rate (which is little changed with age) and the maximum heart rate predicted from the following previously mentioned formula: 220 − age in years = maximum heart rate (Fig 5–8). It has been shown that in older persons, significant conditioning results from activity that utilizes 40% of the heart-rate interval. This effectiveness threshold is lower than that in younger people. In practical terms, this means that a person in his or her 60s can obtain benefit from a daily exercise program involving 30 minutes of walking at a pace sufficient to raise the heart rate to around 105 beats per minute. Greater levels of conditioning result from using more of the available interval. It is prudent, however, to regard 75% of the available range as the "do not exceed" value for unsupervised activity.

In addition to improving physical capacity, conditioning has important side effects:

1. It has been shown to reduce the blood pressure in the hypertensive person, presumably by opening up the vascular bed and lowering peripheral resistance.
2. It is effective in reducing obesity since increasing activity is, for many persons, easier than reducing calorie intake, and moreover, exercise more specifically controls adiposity where weight loss by dietary restriction affects both lean and fat components.

3. It activates intracellular enzyme systems involved in the elimination of oxidizing free radicals.
4. It appears to reduce tension and have a tranquilizing effect probably through the mediation of endorphins.

SUGGESTED READING

Respiratory System
Campbell EJ, Lefrak SS: How aging affects the structure and function of the respiratory system. *Geriatrics* 1978; 33:68–78.
Holland J, Milic-Emili J, Macklem PT: Regional distribution of pulmonary ventilation and perfusion in elderly subjects. *J Clin Invest* 1968; 47:81–82.
Krumpe PE, Knudson RJ, Parsons G, et al: The aging respiratory system. *Clin Geriatr Med*, 1985; 1:143–175.
Lynne-Davies P: Influence of age on the respiratory system. *Geriatr* 1977; 32:57–62.
Mittman C, Edelman NH, Norris AH: Relationship between chest wall and pulmonary compliance and age. *J Appl Physiol* 1965; 20:1211.

Cardiovascular System
Klausner SC, Schwartz AB: The aging heart. *Clin Geriatr Med* 1985; 119–144.
Lakatta EG: Cardiovascular function and age. *Geriatrics* 1987; 42:84–94.
McDermott DJ, Stekiel WJ, Koth LC, et al: Age related changes in cardiovascular responses to diverse circulatory stresses, in Sleight P (ed): *Arterial Baroceptors and Hypertension*. New York, Oxford University Press, 1981, pp 361–364.
Montoye HJ, Willis PW, Howard GE, et al: Cardiac preejection period: Age and sex comparisons. *J Gerontol* 1971; 26:208–216.
Norris AH, Shock NW, Yiengst MJ: Age changes in heart rate and blood pressure responses to tilting and standardized exercises. *Circulation* 1953; 8:521–526.

Physical Activity
Davies CTM: The oxygen transporting system in relation to age. *Clin Sci* 1973; 42:1–13.
DeVries HA: Physiological effects of an exercise training regime upon men aged 52–88. *J Gerontol* 1970; 25:325–336.
Horvath SM, Borgia JF: Cardiopulmonary gas transport and aging. *Am Rev Respir Dis* 1984; 129:568–571.
Larson EG, Bruce RA: Exercise and aging. *Ann Intern Med* 1986; 105:783–785.
Shephard RJ: *Physical Activity and Aging*. London, Croom Helm, 1978.
Shephard RJ: Training for the elderly. *Clin Sports Med* 1986; 5:511–533.

6

The Kidney and the Alimentary Tract

KIDNEY

During development, the kidney undergoes a series of regressions and remodelings that lead through the pronephros and mesonephros to the meta-nephros, which is established before birth. At birth, despite the small size of the organ, a full complement of nephron units has developed, and growth to adult size involves enlargements of the glomeruli and tubules, especially the proximal convoluted segment and the juxtamedullary units, which provide the long loops to the medulla. The adult kidney is capable of compensatory hypertrophy following, for example, the donation of a kidney; this hypertrophy appears to involve an enlargement of the nephron units without a change in their number. There is some evidence that in very young persons this may involve hyperplasia, whereas in older persons, enlargement occurs by hypertrophy. The kidney reaches a maximum size in early adulthood and thereafter loses mass at a rate that increases markedly after age 50 years. Anatomical studies have shown that this age-related loss of mass involves the progressive deletion of entire nephron units, although a small number of aglomerular tubular systems (as many as 3%) have been reported in old kidneys (Fig 6–1).

Both the absolute size and the ratio between size of the glomeruli and the proximal tubules in surviving nephrons remain constant. The observation supports the unit deletion theory and demonstrates that

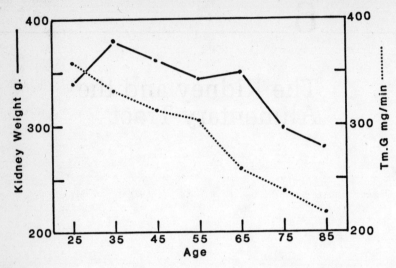

FIG 6–1.
The decline in kidney mass and in tubular maximum for glucose reabsorption (Tm_G). The similarity in the rates of decline supports the notion that age-related loss of renal substance comes about by loss of nephron units. Tm_G values are standardized to a surface area of 1.73 m². (Based on data from Calloway NO, Foley CF, Lagerbloo PJ: *Am Geriatr Soc* 1965; 13:20–28, and Miller JH, McDonald RK, Shock NW: *J Gerontol* 1952; 7:196–200.

the capacity for compensatory hypertrophy is lost with aging of the organ.

The remodeling of the kidney that occurs during development appears to be induced by primary changes in the vasculature, and alterations in the pattern of perfusion have been suggested as the primary cause of the deletion of nephron units seen in aging. The major vascular alteration involves a reduction in the number of glomerular capillary loops, leading to the deletion of both the glomerulus and the associated peritubular plexus. An alternative pattern, seen mainly in juxtamedullary glomeruli, involves the formation of an arteriolar bypass of the degenerated glomerular capillaries (the Isaacs-Ludwig arteriole), which ensures the continued perfusion of the vasa recta of the medulla. Arcuate and interlobar arteries become tortuous, and although smaller arterial vessels show a loss of elastic tissue and a replacement of muscle by collagen, there is very little change in the lumen size. In the renal veins, the development of bundles of longitudinal muscle is a mark of aging; they are absent in children and present in 40% of the vessels of elderly persons. Universally, the basement membrane becomes thickened, and there is an increase in the quantity of connective tissue. This is minor in the cortex but major in the medulla where the large population of interstitial cells is replaced by extracellular material. From age 50 years onward, there is a significant reduction in medullary hydration. These changes in the medullary interstitium, together with the loss of juxtamedullary glomeruli, which provide solute to the medullary osmotic stratification process, and the persistence of vasa recta perfusion, account for the significant loss of concentrating ability in the old kidney.

Kidney weight remains stable from maturity until 40 years of age and then progressively decreases so that by age 80 years, the renal mass is only 70% of the adult value. Renal perfusion, however, is at its maximum in late adolescence, at which time the approximately 360 g of tissue receives 25% of the cardiac output (i.e., 1.25 L/minute). This peak perfusion decreases slowly over the next 5 years and thereafter remains stable until 40 years of age when a major linear decline begins. At age 80 years, perfusion is only 50% of that in the young adult. The glomerular filtration rate follows a similar course of decline but at a somewhat slower rate (Fig 6–2).

This change in the ratio of filtration rate to plasma flow (filtration fraction) may arise from a variety of causes. Since the estimate of the rate of plasma flow is made by measurement of the clearance of para-aminohippuric acid (PAH) or, in earlier studies, by iodopyracet (Diodrast), a reduction in the secretory efficiency of the proximal tubules could give rise to a falsely low estimate of the plasma flow. Direct measurements of the arteriovenous difference for PAH, however, have

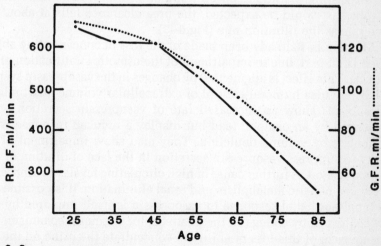

FIG 6–2.
The decline in renal plasma flow (R.P.F.) rate and in glomerular filtration rate (G.F.R.). Values are standardized to a surface area of 1.73 m². (Based on data from Davies DF, Shock NW: *J Clin Invest* 1950; 29:496–507.)

shown no relationship with age. The increase in the filtration fraction, therefore, must be due to some anatomical or physiologic change in the glomerulus. It has been suggested that there is a preferential loss of cortical glomeruli in which the filtration fraction is usually lower than in the juxtamedullary units. Another possible explanation is that there is a shift in the distribution of resistance offered by the glomerular arterioles either by an anatomical change in the lumen size or by a physiologic change in the tone of the arteriolar smooth muscle. One of the few effective means of increasing renal blood flow is by the administration of pyrogen. This technique applied to a group of young, middle-aged, and old subjects has demonstrated that in all three cases, the filtration fraction fell while the glomerular filtration rate remained stable. This indicates that the age-related decrease in the partial functions represents a matched loss of nephrons and vascular elements, and the age-related change in the filtration/perfusion ratio is due, in part, to a reversible alteration in the tone of the glomerular vessels.

Measurements of the maximal rate of secretory transport (Tm) for PAH or of reabsorptive transport for glucose are used to determine the available mass of the proximal tubular epithelium. Both these fall at a rate very close to the filtration rate, which is further confirmation of the loss of function by units (see Fig 6–1). However, the "splay" of these transport processes (the transition from total reabsorption or secretion to the plateau of saturated maximal transport) diminishes with age, suggesting that the nephron population has become more homogeneous. As would be expected, the urea clearance falls at about the same rate as the filtration rate (Fig 6–3).

Mention has already been made of the loss of concentrating ability which is, in part, due to impairment of the osmotic stratification of the medulla. This effect is augmented by changes in the vasopressin system, which provides humoral control of extracellular volume and tonicity. Old subjects show an increased rate of vasopressin secretion when challenged by an osmotic load but display a reduced response when challenged by volume depletion. They also show impairment of the ability to suppress vasopressin secretion in the face of dilution or volume expansion. A further cause of high circulating levels of vasopressin is reduced hepatic metabolism and renal elimination. It is possible that the renal epithelial response to vasopressin is itself impaired by loss of receptors or by change in the postreceptor effector mechanism. The consequence of this loss of ability to concentrate the urine on the one hand, or to excrete "free" osmotically uncommitted water, is a progression toward the condition of isosthenuria as nephrons are lost.

A further factor involved is an impairment of the renin-angiotensin-

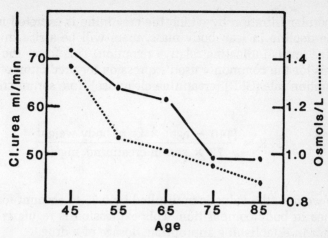

FIG 6–3.
Aging changes in maximal urea clearance and in limiting osmotic concentration of urine. Values for urea clearance are standardized to a surface area of 1.73 m². (Based on data from Lewis WH, Alving AS: Changes with age in the renal function of adult men. *Am J Physiol* 1938; 123:500–515.

aldosterone system that may have its origin in aging of the juxtaglomerular apparatus. Old people have the tendency to develop dilutional hyponaturemia simulating the syndrome of inappropriate vasopressin secretion (SIADH).

   The ability to form and excrete ammonia is reduced, but this appears to be due to the loss of renal mass rather than to a cellular defect in ammoniagenesis. The ability to form titratable acid is not impaired in terms of the hydrogen ion gradient that can be established in the distal tubule. The reduced availability of buffers in the tubule, which is the result of reduced filtration, is countered to a minor extent by the increased distal delivery of phosphate that is brought about by depression of proximal phosphate reabsorption under the influence of elevated circulating levels of parathyroid hormone. The older individual is not at a disadvantage in maintaining acid-base homeostasis under normal load conditions as evidenced by a relatively unchanged blood chemistry. The problem is rather how quickly corrections can be made than in the set-point or target of the correction. This effect is seen in most of the homeostatic mechanisms of the aged.

   It must be borne in mind that renal functions are commonly reported standardized to a body surface area of 1.73 m². Depression of function with age seems to be less if reference is made to lean body mass. In other words, the kidney appears to age in harmony with the metabolism that it serves. An estimate of the body's lean metabolizing mass can be made from the 24-hour excretion of creatinine. If the fall in glomerular filtration by which the creatinine is excreted is greater than the decline in lean body mass, there will be a rise in plasma creatinine levels indicating relative retention. This forms the conceptual basis for the commonly used expression for prediction of glomerular filtration rate (GFR) (creatinine clearance) from serum creatinine, viz

$$\text{GFR} = \frac{(140 - \text{age}) \times \text{kg of body weight}}{72 \times \text{serum creatinine, mg/dl}}$$

For women, the value is multiplied by 0.85 to account for the sex difference in body composition. This expression is regularly used as one factor in establishing appropriate dosage of a drug.

THE ALIMENTARY TRACT

Aging affects the alimentary tract in two major ways: (1) a slowing of the proliferation of the epithelium, and (2) the loss of neurons from the enteric nervous system. This autonomous system consisting of the myenteric plexus and the submucous plexus is responsible for coordination of movement as well as the integration of secretion, absorption, and vascular perfusion. Although the activity of the enteric system is modulated by the autonomic system, it is perfectly capable of controlling the alimentary tract in the absence of central nervous system effects. The system is characterized by the large number of neurons that comprise it (a number in excess of that of neurons in the spinal cord), by the complexity of the neuronal interconnections, and by the variety of neurotransmitters involved. Our understanding of the detailed operation of this system is at present very incomplete.

Throughout the alimentary tract, the integrity of the epithelial surface is maintained by a balance between epithelial cell proliferation and shedding. The rate of turnover of these cells is greater than that of other body cells with the exception of some of the leukocytes. Typically, the rate of turnover falls by about 25% between youth and old age. Perfusion of the gut falls at approximately the same rate as the reduction in cardiac output, about 1% per year after middle adulthood.

THE MOUTH

Aging of the mouth is expressed mainly by loss of teeth with consequent impairment of mastication and the oral phase of swallowing (see Chapter 4). In primitive man, loss of teeth shortened life, but today partial restoration of mastication can be obtained with dentures, albeit at the cost of loss of some taste sensation. After age 50 years, there is a reduction in salivary flow, both resting and stimulated, due perhaps to loss of taste and smell sensations but also to reduction in secretory tissue. Both mucous and serous components are affected; ptyalin content is reduced. Older persons show an increased incidence of salivary calculi.

THE ESOPHAGUS

The aging esophagus undergoes a series of changes sufficiently regular and general to admit the term "presbyesophagus" involving peristaltic and sphincteric function. The act of swallowing begins with relaxation of the upper esophageal sphincter and initiation of a traveling wave of peristalsis. (This is referred to as primary peristalsis in distinction from the secondary type, which clears the esophagus after gastroesophageal reflux). On arrival of the peristaltic wave, the lower esophageal sphincter, which is maintained in a tonic state by humoral and chemical factors, relaxes until the wave has passed through it. In the old person, peristaltic waves are not initiated by every swallow, and furthermore, the lower esophageal sphincter fails to relax with the arrival of each wave. In addition, the lower part of the esophagus shows ringlike contractions that are nonperistaltic (the so-called teritary contractions). Manometric studies have shown that, with age, total motor activity is not reduced but rather becomes uncoordinated. The net result of these changes is a delayed entry of food into the stomach, which is perceived as a sense of substernal fullness. This, for many people, substantially reduces the pleasure of a meal. Furthermore, these impairments of esophageal motility are dangerous in old people who are lying down while eating because of the possibility of aspiration.

Although changes in the esophageal mucosa have not been sufficiently studied, biopsies have shown some reduction of the rete pegs of the epithelial layer with a consequent reduction in the area of the basal germinal layer. In the lower part of the esophagus, the epithelium may undergo metaplasia into a gastric type of columnar epithelium, the condition of Barrett's esophagus. This condition shows a bimodal age distribution with one peak of incidence in youth and a second at 60 to 80 years.

THE STOMACH

The condition of atrophic gastritis, which affects both mucosa and muscle is relatively common in the old. The extent to which this atrophy might be regarded as physiologic is uncertain. The relatively few studies of gastric motility report reduced intensity and frequency of movement and a significant prolongation of gastric emptying time.

The volume of gastric secretion in response to a test meal diminishes after the age of 40 years, a change which is greater in men than women (Fig 6–4). Resting acid secretion or histamine-induced secretion falls from age 50 years onward, again more in males than females. Acid output in response to pentagastrin stimulation is only slightly reduced by aging. Histamine and gastrin bind to different receptor sites, and so this differential response may reflect changes in receptor density or in some postreceptor event. When the test-meal response is standardized for lean body mass or size of the exchangeable potassium pool, the

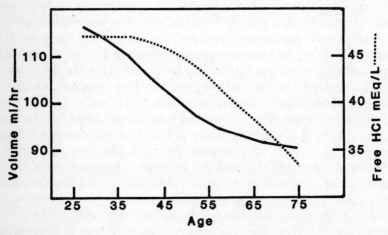

FIG 6–4.
Age-related change in response to a standard test meal. The declines shown occur only in men. In women, while there is a small decline in secretion rate, the concentration of free acid remains constant. (Based on data from Ivy AC, Grossman MI, Digestive system, in Landry AI (ed): *Cowdry's Problems in Aging.* Baltimore, Williams & Wilkins Co, 1952.)

secretion rate remains constant in the male and in fact increases in the female.

Pepsin secretion shows a fall in middle age but then remains constant. The suggestion has been made that in atrophic gastritis, there is a reduction in secretion of intrinsic factor accounting for an age-associated incidence of pernicious anemia, but there is evidence that intrinsic factor continues to be secreted even when acid production is profoundly reduced.

In extreme cases of mucosal aging, gastric glands may be totally lost and the epithelium takes on a duodenal appearance. The cells have an enzyme profile characteristic of the small intestine.

THE SMALL INTESTINE

The length and mass of the small bowel appear to remain constant with age, although some atrophy is believed to occur in the muscular layers. Surface area is significantly diminished; this diminishment is brought about by a reduction in the height of the villi and conversion of the fingerlike shape to a broader more flattened form. There is no evidence that absorption of the major nutrients is impaired in a healthy older person, although such an impairment might be expected as a consequence of the reduction in absorptive surface area and the reduction in perfusion. Carbohydrate absorption is commonly tested by the nonmetabolized sugar D-xylose, which uses the same pathway as the hexose glucose and galactose. Absorption of D-xylose is independent of digestive processes and bile, so the test provides an indication of mucosal integrity and adequacy of perfusion. The conventional test is, however, based on the renal excretion of a dose given by mouth and so, in effect, is a test of both absorption and excretion. The test shows abnormal results in persons over 70 years. When the test is modified so that the absorption is assessed by the concentrations achieved in the blood, it is apparent that absorption remains intact with age.

There is no evidence of impairment of amino acid absorption at least as judged by dietary protein loads up to about twice the typical intake.

Lipid absorption appears to be impaired in older subjects. Similar observations in experimental animals have implicated a defect in the formation of chylomicrons and other lipoproteins and impaired synthesis of apoprotein and phospholipid.

Reduced calcium absorption with age is perhaps related to reduced absorption of vitamin D. Absorption of vitamin B_{12} and of iron shows no relation to age.

THE PANCREAS

Relatively little is known about the effects of age on the human exocrine pancreas, but there appears to be a loss of secretory acini and some enlargement of the ductal system between the ages of 50 and 80 years. There is no drop in weight of the gland, but this may well be due to replacement of active mass by adipose tissue. The secretion of bicarbonate and amylase in response to secretin and cholecystokinin (CCK) stimulation shows a slight fall in older subjects only after protracted stimulation. While it is conceivable that an organ that is called on to perform an enormous quantity and variety of protein synthesis might show some reduced efficiency with age, there is no evidence of an age-dependent impairment of digestive secretions. Although lipid intolerance in the older subject is sometimes attributed to inadequacy of pancreatic lipase secretion, this seems to be unlikely since this enzyme has a tenfold safety factor for dealing with the normal levels of fat in the diet. The pancreas possesses such a large functional reserve that any loss of parenchyma that occurs with age does not compromise digestive function.

THE LIVER

The liver accounts for 2.5% of the body weight in the adult, but weight loss begins around 40 years of age. This reduction in size is linearly progressive so that in the very old, the organ is no more than 1.5% of the body weight. With reduction in the number of hepatocytes, the surviving cells become larger. Multinucleated cells become common, and mitochondrial density is reduced. There is also a reduction in the amount of smooth endoplasmic reticulum and Golgi membrane. Widening of the biliary spaces has also been reported to accompany loss of parenchymal mass.

Tests of liver function using the organic anionic dyes sulfobromophthalein (Bromsulphalein) or indocyanine green have demonstrated that the aging hepatocyte has a reduced storage capacity for the dye but that the maximum secretory transport rate is preserved. Animal studies suggest that the decreased storage capacity is characteristic of the polyploid cells indicating an inverse relationship between storage capacity and the DNA content of the cells.

Liver blood flow declines at the rate of about 1.5% per year from the maximum values seen in the young adult. By age 65 years, the regional perfusion is about 60% of that in the young.

Aging hepatocytes show a markedly reduced proliferative capacity that has been attributed, in part, to a reduced protein synthesis rate. Although the plasma albumin concentration tends to fall with age, the rate of hepatic synthesis appears to be well preserved into the seventh decade. The suggestion can be made that, with age, the "target" for protein synthesis is adjusted to a lower set-point.

The liver is the major organ for metabolism of drugs, and many studies have shown that the overall capacity for drug metabolism declines. While a part of this decline is due to the reduction in regional perfusion, a major factor is the reduced activity of hepatic enzymes, especially the microsomal mixed-function oxidases. Nutritional factors also play a part in hepatic drug metabolism; a case in point is the requirement of adequate levels of vitamin C and folate for the demethylation step of drug metabolism. There is no aging change in the plasma concentrations of bilirubin alkaline phosphatase, serum glutamic oxaloacetic transaminase (SGOT), and serum glutamic pyruvic transaminase (SGPT) nor in the oxidative disposal of ethanol. In these regards, function is unaffected.

THE COLON

Comparison of colonic tissue taken by biopsy or at autopsy from subjects of various ages has shown atrophy of the mucosa, hypertrophy of the muscularis mucosae, and atrophy of the muscular layers to be associated with aging. Weakening of the colonic wall, which in association with high luminal pressures leads to the development of diverticuli, may involve both muscular atrophy and changes in collagen. Another factor may be incoordination of movement due to loss of enteric nerve cells, such that the longitudinal muscle fails to relax when the circular muscle contracts. The constipation of old age is of multifactorial origin. Loss of muscle tone and motor activity in the colon, a low-fiber diet, a rise in the threshold of stimulation for initiation of defecation reflexes, and damage by laxative abuse all contribute.

SUGGESTED READING

Kidney

Agarwal BM, Cabebe FG: Renal acidification in elderly subjects. *Nephron* 1980; 26:291–295.

Brown WW, Spry L, David BB: Alterations in renal homeostasis with aging, in Davis BB, Wood WG: *Homeostatic Function and Aging.* New York, Raven Press, 1985.

Calloway NO, Foley CF, Langerbloom P: Uncertainties in geriatric data. II. Organ Size. *J Am Geriatr Soc* 1965; 13:20–28.

Epstein M: Effects of aging on the kidney. *Fed Proc* 1979; 38:168–172.

Kaysen CA, Myers BD: The aging kidney. *Clin Geriatr Med* 1985; 1:207–222.

Lindeman RD: Age changes in renal function, in Goldman R, Rickstein M (eds): *Physiology and Pathology of Human Aging.* New York, Academic Press, 1975.

Papper S: The effects of age in reducing renal function. *Geriatrics* 1973; 28:83–98.

Rowe JW, Andres R, Tobin JD, et al: The effect of age on creatinine clearance in man: A cross-sectional and longitudinal study. *J Gerontol* 1976; 31:155–163.

Alimentary Tract

Calloway NO, Merrill RS: The aging adult liver. *J Am Geriatr Soc* 1965; 13:594–598.

Geokas MC, Coneas DN, Majumdar APN: The aging gastrointestinal tract, liver and pancreas. *Clin Geriatr Med* 1985; 1:177–205.

Gullo L, Priori P, Daniele C, et al: Exocrine pancreatic function in the elderly. *Gerontology* 1983; 29:407–411.

Hollis JE, Castell DO: Esophageal function in elderly man: A new look at prebyesophagus. *Ann Intern Med* 1974; 80:371–374.

James OFW: Gastrointestinal and liver function in old age. *Clin Gastroenterol* 1983; 12:671–691.

Soregel KH, Zboralske FF, Amberg JR: Presbyesophagus: Esophageal motility in nonagenarians. *J Clin Invest* 1964; 43:1472–1479.

7

The Nervous System

ANATOMICAL AGING OF THE BRAIN

The weight of the brain reaches its peak of approximately 1.4 kg in the early 20s and then undergoes a slow decline. By age 80 years, the loss reaches 7%, or about 100 g. This weight loss is accompanied by a reduction in the cortical area brought about by the broadening of sulci and a flattening of the gyri. This change is most apparent in the anterior halves of the hemispheres. There is a small increase in the size of the ventricles. Studies of hemispheric volume have shown a faster rate of loss in men than in women. During the aging process, the ratio of gray to white matter changes, indicating that there is some differential loss of cells and fibers. The ratio declines from ages 20 to 50 years (predominant loss of cells) and then increases with further aging (predominant loss of fibers) (Fig 7–1). The hydration of brain tissue increases after age 70 years but may decline again in the very old.

Throughout life, neurons are lost, and it has been estimated that the rate of loss is about 50,000 per day out of a total of 10 billion. The rate of loss is highest during the period of brain development and is a part of the normal process of modeling of the adult circuitry. Alarming though the figures for rate of loss of neurons may appear at first, it, in fact, amounts to approximately a 3% loss over a lifetime.

Cells are lost from the cerebral cortex at a rate that varies widely from area to area. The Golgi type II cells are particularly affected, and the pyramidal cells of layer 3 lose the horizontal association dendrites. In some areas, cell loss may be as great as 20% to 40%. The greatest

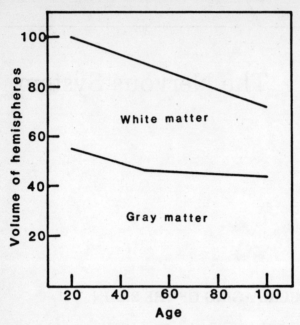

FIG 7–1.
Differing rates of loss of gray and white matter in the cerebral hemispheres. (Based on data from Terry RD: Physical changes of the aging brain, in Behnke JA, Finch CE, Moment GB [eds]: *Biology of Aging.* New York, Plenum Press, 1978, p 208.)

loss occurs in the superior temporal gyrus, the precentral gyrus, and the area striata. The postcentral gyrus loses few or no cells. A similar loss occurs in the cerebellum but is later in onset than that in the cerebrum. The nuclei of the brain stem show no age-related loss of cells, with the exception of the locus ceruleus, where the loss begins only after age 65 years.

In the peripheral nerves, there are fewer large fibers, and this is especially marked in the lumbosacral dorsal roots (Fig 7–2). Likewise, in the efferent system, the largest efferent fibers are lost. The consequences of this shift in the spectrum of fiber size are the slight change (5%) in the conduction velocity and the appearance of prolonged (polyphasic) muscle action potentials recorded with the electromyogram (EMG) (Fig 7–3).

CELLULAR CHANGES

Significant changes occur in both the neurons and in the glial cells. The major change affecting the axons is neuroaxonal degeneration, which is characterized by a loss of myelin and swellings on the axis cylinders. This slow degenerative process, often referred to as a "dying back," can be observed in 30% of older persons, especially in the posterior column system.

Changes in the neuronal cell bodies take the form of inclusions and changes in microtubule structure. The most common inclusion is the autofluorescent "aging pigment" lipofuscin. This pigment appears to be accumulated as a continuous process. It appears first as diffusely distributed fine granules that then become clumped, often in perinuclear sites. There appears to be a variety of lipofuscins since cells in different areas of the brain have pigment of differing ultrastructure. Animal studies have shown that the amount of pigment accumulation can be modified by dietary vitamin E; deficient diet produces increased deposition. These observations support the notion that the pigment is the product of peroxidation of structural elements.

Irregular membrane-bounded accumulations of protein fibrils occur commonly in the cells of the thalamus and brain stem. In the melanin-containing cells of the midbrain and brain stem, there are homogeneous

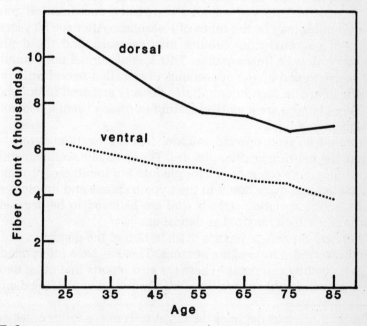

FIG 7–2.
Aging change in fiber count in dorsal and ventral roots (eighth thoracic segment). (Based on data from Corbin KB, Gardner ED: Decrease in number of myelinated fibers in human spinal roots with age. *Anat Rec* 1937; 68:63.)

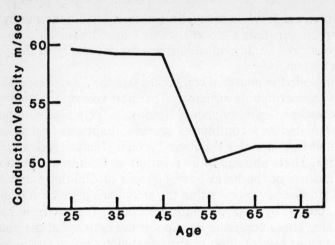

FIG 7–3.
Effect of age on conduction velocity in the ulnar nerve. (Based on data from Wagman IH, Leese HJ, *Neurophysiol* 1952; 15:235.)

hyaline bodies (Lewy bodies) 10 to 20 mµ (diameter) with fine radiating strands. Cells of the hippocampus undergo granulovacuolar degeneration in which clusters of vacuoles surround a dense central granule. These vacuoles may be the relics of lysosomes. After age 60 years, the number of neuronal microtubules may decrease, and the depletion thereafter follows a linear course. This loss of normal microtubules is often accompanied by the appearance of so-called neurofibrillary tangles, which are, in fact, microtubules densely arranged in double helices. These tangles are a marked feature in cases of senile dementia of the Alzheimer's type.

From age 60 years onward, rounded foci of interstitial degeneration develop, the neuritic (senile) plaques. These may be scattered and solitary, or they may coalesce. These plaques are found most commonly in the cortex and more rarely in the hypothalamus and limbic system; they have fine radiating strands that are believed to be degenerated dendrites on which amyloid is deposited.

There are numerous reports of distortion of the dendrites and loss of dendritic spines from aging neurons. This has been interpreted as a change preceding cell death. There are also reports that other neurons display a considerable dendritic plasticity and an expanding dendritic field as they age.

Death of neurons depletes the target cells of synaptic contacts, and surviving adjacent neurons may display "reactive synaptogenesis" by axonal sprouting, potentially restoring the circuit that was lost. The process occurs after brain damage and may be a way in which the aging brain compensates for loss of neurons.

The glial cells, which have responsibility for maintaining the extracellular environment for the neurons and serve as middlemen in metabolic exchanges, also undergo aging change. Glial hypertrophy has been reported, especially in synaptic fields. Cell volume is increased, but there appears to be no change in the number of astrocytes; there is some decline in oligodendrocyte count.

Fibrillary astrocytes become more prominent with age, and the cells attach to blood vessels by enlarged foot processes. The substance amylopectin appears in the astrocytic processes in the form of the corpora amylacea. These bodies have a dense central core with a fibrillar border and are found most commonly in the immediate subpial cortex and near the linings of the ventricles. Within the choroid plexus, fibrils appear in both the epithelial cells and the ependymal cells. Especially prominent in the basal ganglia is an increase in the size of the perivascular space and a thickening of the walls of the small arteries.

CEREBRAL BLOOD FLOW

In the young adult, the perfusion of the brain occurs at a rate of 50 to 60 ml/minute/100 g of tissue; a little less than 40 ml/minute/100 g is regarded as the necessary minimum to maintain full neuronal function. This marginal level of blood flow is approached in the very old, since the rate decreases 20% over the age span of 30 to 70 years. The vertebral arteries tend to become tortuous with aging due to changes in the vertebrae and intervertebral disks and may become kinked with movements of the neck. This obstruction together with the already parlous perfusion may precipitate one variety of the transient ischemic attack to which many old persons are prone. Cerebral oxygen consumption appears to be better maintained than blood flow so that the arteriovenous oxygen difference increases. Studies of glucose utilization by brain indicates that, on a tissue weight basis, this too is well maintained.

NEUROTRANSMISSION

The process of neurotransmission involves synthesis, axonal transport, storage, release, and disposal of the transmitter by the presynaptic element and engagement of the appropriate receptor postsynaptically. Each stage of this process is potentially affected by aging, and it is the cumulative effect of these changes that manifests itself in the slowing of central processing over multisynaptic pathways in the old. This increase in synaptic delay is superimposed on a reduced velocity of conduction of the nerve impulse that in large fibers may fall by 25% between the 20s and age 80 years.

Nerve cells have a vigorous synthetic function in addition to maintaining their property of excitability. The products of this synthesis include protein, the specific neurotransmitter substances, enzymes involved in the metabolism of neurotransmitters, and substances that modulate structural changes in the nerve cell of origin as well as in adjacent glia cells and other neurons that they contact at the synapses. The substances are synthesized within the nerve cell body and then travel along the axons for considerable distances, in excess of 1 m in some cases. The process involved in this movement of material is active, utilizing energy, and is termed axonal transport (AxT). Different substances are transported at very different rates. Some only travel 1 to 2 mm/day, others 400 mm/day, while a few move rapidly at a rate around 2 m/day. Axonal transport has the responsibility for maintaining the supply of neurotransmitters at the axon termination as well as providing structural material at the synaptic membrane. In addition, AxT has what is termed a neurotropic role in regulating activity and probably functions transsynaptically in the target cells of the nerve. Axonal transport can also occur in the reverse direction from axon termination towards the cell body. By this means, the synaptic connection may be able to influence events in both the presynaptic and postsynaptic (target) nerve cells.

In the experimental animal, studies have shown major changes in AxT with aging, with the rate of transport falling by a factor of as much as ten. Impairment of AxT has been shown to be a fundamental change in diseases characterized by peripheral degeneration of nerve fibers as well as in the loss of nerve cells in the cerebellum that are the target of some nerve pathways. It is tempting to speculate that some of the typical aging loss of synapses and neurons has its origins in impaired AxT.

Changes in the metabolism of neurotransmitter substances have profound effects on both behavioral and regulatory systems. The cholinergic system has received major attention because of its involvement in memory and in disorders such as parkinsonism and Alzheimer's disease. Changes have been reported in the synthetic and disposal systems. Choline acetyltransferase activity decreases, and there is a less significant increase in acetylcholinesterase activity. The net result is a reduction in acetylcholine concentration in the brain, but this has not been studied directly since it is too labile for postmortem examination. The loss of acetyltransferase activity is most marked in the cortex and in the caudate nucleus. This latter is the site of the major pathology of the strongly age-related disease, Huntington's chorea. Studies in the experimental animal have shown reductions in muscarinic receptor binding in these same two areas.

A limited number of studies in humans have shown that the level of enzymes concerned with catecholamine synthesis decreases with age, while the major enzyme involved in the disposal of the catecholamines, monoamine oxidase (MAO), increases in concentration in several parts of the brain. The concentration of norepinephrine in the hindbrain falls 40% to 50% between young adulthood and age 70 years. More extensive and detailed studies in experimental animals have confirmed this human evidence and further have shown that these changes in catecholamine synthesis occur in specific groups of cells. This implies that only some pathways are susceptible to change with aging. Catecholamines are involved as transmitters in the hypothalamic neurosecretion of releasing factors, especially the gonadotropin releasing factors. Since the liberation of releasing factors is modulated by the circulating levels of pituitary or other hormones, it has been speculated that catecholamine synthesis in certain hypothalamic sites is itself controlled by these hormones. A defect in this feedback system could then arise from an age-related change in the receptors of the synthesizing cells.

The demonstration of elevated levels of monoamine oxidase in the aged has led to experimentation with MAO inhibitors (such as procaine hydrochloride) as an "elixir of youth." The results of such trials have been largely negative.

It is well established that parkinsonism is associated with a reduction in the amount of the monoamine dopamine in the basal ganglia. Dopamine is the neurotransmitter that provides communication between the cells of the substantia nigra and the corpus striatum. The occurrence of parkinsonism is strongly related to age, and the tremor and shuffling gate of the old may well be lesser manifestations of this defect. Fortunately, "replacement therapy" is possible and is at least partially effective. L-Dopa (levodopa), which can cross the blood-brain barrier, is converted in the brain into dopamine and norepinephrine. Other palliative approaches to this disease use monoamine oxidase inhibitors (especially the inhibitor of the β-oxidase, which is found in the brain and not in the periphery) and the dopaminergic agonist bromocriptine.

There is a progressive fall in dopamine binding sites with age, and a similar change affects β-adrenergic sites. It has also been suggested that reduced β-receptor responsiveness may be due to changes in membrane fluidity affecting the receptor-adenylate cyclase coupling.

Glutamine acid decarboxylase, which is responsible for the formation of γ-aminobutyric acid (GABA) from the precursor glutamic acid, undergoes a widespread though modest decline, which is most marked in the thalamus. This has led to speculation concerning the role of GABA cells in the processing of sensory information. Little is presently known about the age-related alteration of other putative neurotransmitters in man.

AGING OF REFLEXES

At the segmental level of spinal organization, the simple stretch reflexes are often depressed, and evidence from experimental animals has revealed a progressive increase in the central delay of these monosynaptic reflexes. The Achilles tendon reflex is absent or elicited only with reinforcement in a large percentage of older people. Although this central delay may be due to changes in the motor neuron itself, it could also arise from alterations in the input to the motor neurons from descending pathways. The plantar flexion and superficial abdominal reflexes also show an increase in central delay, often of considerable magnitude (e.g., 100 msec). Such changes in central delay, especially if cumulated over complex pathways, could account for a large part of the slowed motor response of old subjects, as tested, for example, by finger tapping.

REACTION TIME

Reaction time is measured as the interval between the presentation of a visual or auditory signal and a motor response, such as pressing a button to terminate the signal. Reaction time thus encompasses the time involved in transduction of the signal, conduction to the central nervous system, processing, and initiation and conduction of a signal out to the appropriate responding muscle group (Fig 7–4). If an EMG is recorded from the muscles involved, the time taken to make the motor response can be determined. Furthermore, the efferent conduction time can be estimated from a separate experiment to measure the conduction velocity of impulses in the motor nerve. Overall reaction time is longer by about 30% in old subjects (230 msec vs. 170 msec).

In part, this is due to a small reduction in the conduction velocity—approximately 2 msec. The "motor time" (time from the start of muscle activation as seen in the EMG to the completion of movement) is prolonged in the older subject, probably due to less muscle power moving the finger slower. Joint stiffness also contributes to this effect. By far the greatest change, however, occurs in the central stages of processing. When motivation is provided by the threat of electric shock delivered at a fixed interval after the stimulus, the age difference is slightly but not significantly reduced. Contributing to the lengthened central time in old subjects is probably an increase in synaptic delay time. In the rat, this increases 40% between young and old. Aging effects are magnified when the reaction task is complicated by a requirement for a decision or if the test is conducted in a less than ideal environment.

CUTANEOUS SENSE

As part of the aging changes in the skin, there is a loss of encapsulated receptors and of Merkel's disks, but there is no apparent loss of free nerve endings. Pressure, touch, and tactile discrimination are impaired, but the most gross alteration is in vibratory sense. This is especially marked in the toes (a tenfold decrement) and somewhat less in the fingers.

Pain and thermal sense are both diminished despite the fact that there is no loss of the free nerve endings of C fibers. Although this decrement may reflect non-neural changes in the skin, there is a real alteration in the threshold of stimulation. In the case of thermal sense, this produces a broadening of the perceived thermal "neutral zone" and impairment of the appropriate behavioral responses to environmental temperature. The increased threshold of pain sensation is reversed in the very old, perhaps because excessive thinning of the skin allows a greater number of nerve endings to be stimulated.

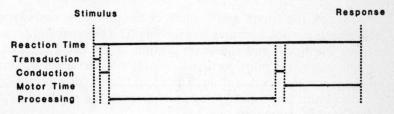

FIG 7–4.
Components of reaction time.

PROPRIOCEPTIVE SENSE

Older persons require greater angular movements at the joints for perception to be achieved; this is especially true of the lower limb. Tests calling for duplication of forced movements show a marked loss of accuracy. The source of this impairment may lie in the number of surviving joint receptors, in reception threshold, in loss of nerve fibers, or in changes in the analyzer component. A contribution may also be made by the physical stiffening of the joint capsule, but it is likely that the major part of the sensory loss is due to deterioration of the posterior columns.

THE SPECIAL SENSES

The analysis of the aging changes in the special senses must take into account the complex sequence of events that ultimately result in the event of perception. First, information is obtained from the environment; then occurs transduction of this information into the common electrical signal of sensation; finally, the propagation of the action potential signal over nerve fibers and through synapses into the central nervous system for processing. The processing of the information involves comparison of the current signal with prior information stored as a memory. Alterations in hearing and vision are among the earliest aging changes of which the person becomes aware. Typically, the course of impairment is linear with age and with an onset of childhood or early adulthood. Contributing to the sensory losses are changes in both the physical and neuronal elements of the sensory system; each of these changes may be minor in itself, but the cumulation of serial impairments produces a major sensory loss. It is convenient to trace these changes from the outside inward to the final stage of perception.

Hearing

With age, the length and breadth of the pinna increases, and the cartilaginous portion becomes less flexible. The external auditory meatus loses elasticity, and the outer portion of the canal narrows and becomes somewhat more tortuous. Secretion of cerumen diminishes and the cerumen becomes drier. The accumulation of wax, which is a not uncommon cause of hearing loss, is more the result of hygienic neglect than functional change.

The tympanic membrane becomes more rigid and occasionally

thickened, although it is common for there to be an increased translucency that changes the landmarks visible to otoscopic examination. There is an increased rigidity of the ossicular chain due to aging of the ossicular ligaments and degeneration of the articulations. Loss of muscle fibers from the tensor and levator veli palatini and the salpingopharyngeal muscles impairs the function of the eustachian canal in providing pressure equalization in the middle ear.

Both Reissner's membrane and the basilar membrane become stiffer as a result of connective tissue changes and, in the case of the basilar membrane, lipid deposition. Atrophy of the stria vascularis is common, impairing both the formation of endolymph and metabolic support of the inner ear structures. There is significant loss of hair cells, both inner and outer, of the organ of Corti and loss of supporting cells. The loss begins in childhood in the basal turn and rises progressively to involve the whole length of the cochlea. There is a gradual loss of ganglion cells and fibers of the auditory nerve, and neurons are lost throughout the auditory pathway, loss being especially marked in the superior temporal gyrus and in the parietal association area.

The auditory orienting reflex becomes slower and less accurate with age, contributing perhaps to the confusion that some of the old display in a multiperson conversation.

Hearing is at its most efficient, in both acuity and range of perceivable frequencies, at age 10 years. At that age, one can hear sounds with frequencies as high as 20 kHz; by age 50 years, this upper limit is only 14 kHz, and by age 60 years, there is little useful hearing above 5 kHz (Fig 7–5). This decline in sensitivity for the higher frequencies is observed in testing by both air and bone conduction; testing locates this impairment central to the outer or middle ear. Shrinkage of the frequency range is accompanied by loss of acuity (amounting to 40 to 50 dB) for all frequencies higher than 1,000 Hz (Fig 7–6). Although pure-tone hearing in the speech frequency range is only moderately attenuated, there is a loss of speech perception much greater than might be predicted, which is attributable perhaps to changes in the central processing of the signals. Auditory reaction times are increased, and there is some loss of sound orientation suggesting poor central processing.

In some persons, with the loss of pure-tone perception, "noise" develops in the auditory circuitry, producing the persistent ringing sensation of tinnitus. More rarely, the elevation of the threshold for hearing is accompanied by an enhanced "recruitment" of perceived intensity after the threshold has been reached. In extreme cases, this

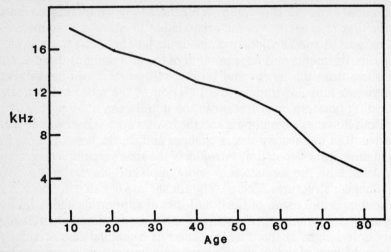

FIG 7–5.
Age-related change in maximum audible frequency (measured at submaximal intensity). (Based on data from Schober FW: Über die Abhängigkeit der oberen Mörgrensse vom Lebensalter. *Acustica* 1952; 4:219.)

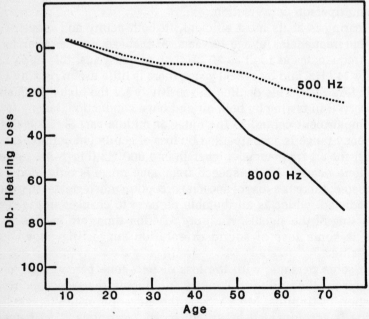

FIG 7–6.
Differential loss of auditory acuity for low and higher frequencies. (Based on data from Lebo CP, Redell RC: The presbycusis component in occupational hearing loss. *Laryngoscope* 1972; 82:1399–1409.)

may result in pain as a consequence of amplifying sound into the audible range.

Evaluation of the extent to which hearing loss is a time-aging change is made difficult by the fact that environmental noise, when sufficiently intense or prolonged, can lead to deafness and the effects of dietary factors or exposure to ototoxic drugs cannot be adequately assessed. The term presbycusis is commonly applied to any hearing loss occurring in the elderly; a more rigid definition restricts the term to a progressive bilaterally symmetrical sensorineural loss.

Vision

The sense of vision is affected by several of the common changes in the body's supporting tissues. With aging, there is a loss of retroorbital fat that leads to recession of the eye. Loss of elastic tissue of the brow and the upper lid leads to ptosis and occlusion of the upper visual field. Loss of elastic tissue in the lower lid may allow the lid to fall forwards separating the lid from the eye and interfering with the normal siphoning of tears. Tear production diminishes so that "dry eye" may result.

With time, the cornea becomes more spherical so that the major axis of astigmatism, which is vertical in youth, becomes horizontal. The cornea and the conjunctiva become thinned, possibly a consequence of ischemia, and this thinning may proceed to the point where the cornea shows folds. There is some loss of the peripheral corneal endothelium, and this, by allowing for fluid exchange, can lead to corneal edema and hazing.

The anterior chamber becomes shallower as a result of thickening of the lens posing a danger of an acute closed-angle glaucoma when the pupil is dilated. The diameter of the pupil, at a maximum in the early teens, follows a linear decline to a minimum at age 60 years. Changes in the fibrous framework of the iris fixes the pupil at this small size and substantially impairs the amount of light admitted. At age 60 years, the amount of light reaching the retina is only one third of that at age 20 years with a consequent rise in threshold for light perception as well as in the level of illumination necessary for reading. The "fixation" of pupillary size reduces the pupillary adjustment to changed levels of illumination. The aqueous humor that is produced at a normal rate tends to develop a yellow autofluorescent pigmentation. This leads to a blue-green color confusion.

Opacities sited at the posterior pole of the lens are relatively common, and this further reduces access of light along the optic axis. The

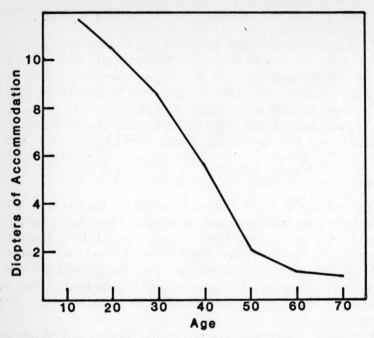

FIG 7–7.
Age-related alteration in the available range of accommodation. (Based on data from Frie-denwald JS: The eye, in Lansing Al [ed]: *Cowdry's Problems in Aging,* Baltimore, Williams & Wilkins Co, 1952.)

decline in lens metabolism accompanying the thickening of the lens and the poorer circulation of the nutritive aqueous may result in the lens imbibing fluid and becoming swollen. This increases the dioptric power of the lens and reverses the normal shift to hyperopia seen in presbyopia. The subjective observation in an older person that reading glasses are no longer necessary is a sign of the impaired lens metabolism and a harbinger of a cataract.

The condition of presbyopia, the loss of range of accommodation for near vision, is perhaps the best known age-related change of the senses (Fig 7–7). The change is essentially a loss of flexibility of the lens, which fails to change shape appropriately when the tension of the suspensory ligaments decreases with the contraction of the ciliary muscle. The lens continues to grow but more slowly throughout life, and between ages 20 and 80 years, the anterior-posterior diameter of the lens increases by 50%. Growth consists of the laying down of new cells on the surface of the lens. At the same time, the central cells lose their cellular identity and become crystalline. In this now acellular part of the lens, micro-opacities develop. Although these do not affect visual acuity, they produce a "dusty windshield" effect, and small bright light sources produce dazzle. This continuing growth of the lens results in not only a loss of lens flexibility but also a reduction in the size of the anterior chamber and some consequent impairment of the circulation of aqueous humor leading to increased intraocular pressure. The aging individual becomes aware of the loss of accommodation by a very obvious change in the distance from the eye at which type can be read. This "near-point," which is about 10 cm at age 20 years, recedes to 100 cm by age 70 years. In addition, the speed with which accommodation is performed declines, due probably to the loss of contractile force in the ciliary muscle or a change in the motor control of the muscle.

The vitreous body loses hydration, and the concentric sheets that provide the skeleton for the mucoid component tend to separate. This may lead to a loss of the important tampon function of the vitreous on the retina and the appearance of "floaters" in the visual field.

Receptors are lost, chiefly affecting the rods of the peripheral retina. This loss, together with a sinking of the eye into the orbit and some degree of ptosis, significantly reduces the size of the visual field. There is a minor loss of receptors of the fovea sufficient to produce a loss of visual acuity even after correction for the aging changes of refraction. The chemical processes of vision become impaired so that dark adaptation occurs more slowly and to a lesser extent.

In the old person, there is a decrease in the "critical fusion frequency"—that is, the least frequency of a flashing light that is perceived as an uninterrupted signal. This effect indicates a longer persistence of the "trace" of the stimulus in the old.

The electroretinogram remains normal in its time relationships but shows a reduction in voltage reflecting the reduced number of active neurons.

Taste

With age, the taste papillae degenerate, and the number of taste buds within each papilla is reduced. Some reports have placed the loss as high as 70% between childhood and age 80 years. Studies using the conventional battery of test substances—sugar, salt, hydrochloric acid, and quinine—have produced results that are divided almost equally between a significant increase in the taste threshold and no change. However, tests in which a controlled galvanic current was used to stimulate receptors (the current produces a metallic or acid taste) have demonstrated a rather linear increase in the threshold beginning in young adulthood and climaxing with a fivefold decrease in sensitivity by age 80 years. The loss of taste sensation is also exacerbated by the reduced saliva flow and reduced amylase content.

The impairment of taste sensation has a number of significant side effects. The body loses an important protective mechanism. Many noxious substances—spoiled food, some drugs, household cleaning materials, etc.—produce a prompt reflex rejection that protects against accidental ingestion. Additionally, eating pleasure is diminished, effecting major nutritional consequences in which the preparatory phases of digestive secretion are impaired. In addition, reduction in the sense of sweetness or saltiness often leads to excessive use of refined sugar or salt, both of which are undesirable changes in the diet of the elderly. Some of the positive side effects of the taste sensation can be regained by the appropriate use of herbs.

Smell

There is anatomical evidence of an age-related loss of neurons in the olfactory bulb, but few systematic tests of olfactory sensitivity have been made. One such study showed a marked age-related elevation of the detection threshold for four common odors—coffee, oil of peppermint, oil of almonds, and coal tar.

Even more striking than the change in olfactory thresholds is failure of identification of specific odors, which becomes especially marked after 60 years of age. The sense of smell shares with taste a protective function and a role in the anticipatory phases of digestion.

The suggestion has been made that the losses in audition, olfaction, and gustation have a common component in neuronal degeneration in the lower part of the postcentral gyrus where the sensations are appreciated.

VESTIBULAR FUNCTION

The vestibular apparatus of old persons shows a significant loss of hair cells of the cristae ampullaris as well as a loss of supporting cells. Degeneration of the macula has also been described in both the saccule and utricle. However, tests of vestibular function, both by the caloric test and by rotation, have given confusing results. In both tests, assessment of vestibular function is based on parameters of the induced nystagmus—duration, amplitude, and frequency. There have been reports of age-related reductions in sensitivity, age-related increases, and a total lack of relation to age. However, when assessment is based on the maximum values for velocity, amplitude, or frequency of the induced nystagmus, the greatest sensitivity is found in middle-aged persons, with lesser sensitivity in young adults and older persons. These tests do not necessarily address the effects of age on the vestibular input to balance and posture, since central integration and processing are not involved to the same extent in the production of nystagmus. Old persons certainly appear to be more resistant than the young adult to motion sickness. As would be expected, older subjects who report bouts of dizziness do not exhibit a reduced vestibular response.

Balance and Posture

The precision with which the motor system can maintain a stable posture is commonly judged by the extent of "sway" of the body when the person is standing with eyes closed. Old people show exaggerated sway. The more demanding test of maintaining balance while standing on one leg is impossible for many of the elderly. Contributing to this impairment of balance are the loss of proprioceptive input, both conscious and unconscious, the loss of cells from the cerebellum, and probably some loss of vestibular input because of the degenerative changes of the saccule and the utricle. The standing posture is less erect than in the young due to loss of muscle power in the trunk and in the extensor of the leg. The tendency for the body's center of gravity to shift forward is "compensated" by some flexion at the knee.

Gait

The gait of an old person tends to be slow, often on a widened base, and shuffling rather than one with the brisk heel-and-toe action typical of youth. Loss of muscle mass and power, changes in the pattern of activation of muscle groups that follow the loss of large motor nerve fibers, and the stiffening of joints all combine with the impairment of proprioceptive sense to produce this picture.

Tremor

Tremor may arise from many changes within the nervous system. The resting tremor of parkinsonism has been identified as resulting from an inadequacy of the transmitter substance dopamine in the nigrostriatal system. The incidence of this condition is strongly related to age. Tremor may also arise from damage to the comparator function of the cerebellum. This "intention tremor," which is part of the general phenomenon of dysmetria, follows the loss of adequate proprioceptive input as well as the loss of cerebellar neurons. All persons, when asked to maintain a limb in a steady position, for example, show some degree of tremor. This is often referred to as "physiologic tremor." In children, the dominant frequency of the tremor is close to 6 Hz. This increases to approximately 10 Hz in the adult and then with further aging falls again to the childhood value. One explanation proposed for this decreased frequency is a central synchronization of motor activity. In old people, clonus can be more readily elicited than in the young. This response to the maintained stretch of a muscle has been attributed to decreased serotonin activity within the olivodentate system.

The general picture of the aging nervous system is declining efficiency involving both the transducer system of receptors (e.g., the thickening lens and sclerosing ossicles of the ear) and the nervous system elements themselves. A reduction in the number of both central and peripheral neurons limits the flow of information in the system, and the remaining elements must transmit signals for a longer time to allow for summation to the threshold level. This, repeated at each stage of a complex information channel, accounts for the increased central processing time that occurs. Furthermore, a reduced number of neurons within the system decreases the functional reserve, thus leading potentially to information overload and confusion of signals. In addition, the aged nervous system requires more time to "clear the decks" to take up a new response (reflected, for example, in the change in the critical fusion frequency). An old person is at a disadvantage when speed is called for in a receptive task. This topic arises again in relation to the higher cortical functions that are discussed in Chapter 11.

SUGGESTED READING

Brody M: An examination of cerebral cortex and brain stem aging, in Terry RD, Gershon S (eds): *Neurobiology of Aging.* New York, Raven Press, 1976, pp 177–182.

Corso JF: *Aging Sensory Systems and Perceptions.* New York, Praeger Publishers, 1981.

Cotman CW, Scheff SW: Compensatory synapse growth in aged animals after neuronal death. *Mech Ageing Dev* 1979; 9:103–117.

Dravid AR: Axonal transport. *Triangle* 1979; 18:117–121.

Fujishima M, Omae T: Brain blood flow and mean transit time as related to aging. *Gerontology* 1980; 26:104–107.

Hanley T: Neuronal fallout in the aging brain: A critical review of the quantitative data. *Age Ageing* 1974; 3:133–151.

Keeney AH, Keeney VT: A guide to examining the aging eye. *Geriatrics* 1980; 35:81–91.

Mullch Q, Peterman W: Influence of age on results of vestibular function tests. *Ann Otol Rhinol Laryngol* 1979; 88:(suppl 56).

Nabol JB: The aging peripheral hearing mechanism, in Beasley DS, Davis GA (eds): *Aging Communication Processes and Disorders.* New York, Grune & Stratton, 1981.

Nerbonne MA: The effects of aging on auditory structures and functions, in Shadden BB: *Communication Behavior and Aging.* Baltimore, Williams & Wilkins, 1988.

Roth GS: Changes in hormone/neurotransmitter action during aging, in Davis BB, Wood WB: *Homeostatic Function and Aging.* New York, Raven Press, 1985.

Vernadakis A: The aging brain. *Clin Geriatr Med* 1985; 1:61–94.

8

The Endocrine System

The endocrine system is central to so many of the body's regulatory and adaptive mechanisms that it is tempting to postulate a major role in the loss of homeostatic competence in the aged to alterations in the endocrine glands. At one time, similarities between aged persons and persons with hypothyroidism led to the false identification of the gland as the seat of aging. Such similarities as do exist—such as, reduced basal metabolic rate, drying of the skin, loss of hair from the outer third of the eyebrows, slowing of mental processes—are quite independent of thyroid function, which is well maintained in health. Apart from the hormonal changes that accompany menopause in the female, age-related functional changes in the endocrine system are, in general, quite subtle and involve not only the glands themselves but also the hypothalamic releasing factors and receptor sites in the target tissues. Often, it is only by challenges to these "higher" or "lower" levels that changes in regulation can be discerned.

PITUITARY

In humans, the pituitary does not lose a significant amount of weight with aging, but there is a reduction of vascularity and an increase in the content of connective tissue. The eosinophil cells (concerned with growth hormone and prolactin production) decrease in number, while the chromophobe cells proliferate.

Growth Hormone.—The amount of growth hormone in the anterior pituitary does not change with age. Studies on the effect of aging on circulating levels of the hormone are complicated by sex differences and by the blunted secretion in obese subjects. Old persons do not show the bursts of secretion during sleep that are seen in young persons, and this has been correlated with the loss of the slow-wave sleep pattern in the old. In old subjects, exercise fails to provoke secretion, and provocative tests using either insulin hypoglycemia or arginine injection, likewise, show a reduced response, but the response can be shifted toward normal by levodopa (L-dopa) administration. This suggests that an impairment exists at the level of the hypothalamic, catecholamine-mediated drive.

Prolactin.—The pituitary content of prolactin is higher in post-menopausal women than in men, but in both sexes, the circulating levels are in the normal range. The values tend to fall in postmenopausal women and to rise in older men. Secretion in response to provocation, for example, by thyrotropin releasing hormone, results in the normal rise, but this rise persists longer in the older subject.

Thyrotropin.—There appears to be no age-related change in the plasma level of thyrotropin. When the secretory response to synthetic releasing hormone is tested, the response to a given dose is significantly lower in old subjects. This may reflect either a reduced sensitivity of the system to the releasing factor or an absolute reduction in secretory capacity.

Corticotropin.—No change occurs in the pituitary content of adrenocorticotropic hormone (ACTH) with age; the circadian rhythm of circulating levels shows no change, and the release in response to stress remains intact. Test results of feedback suppression of secretion by circulating steroids (the dexamethasone suppression test) also show no age-related change.

FSH and LH.—Levels of follicle stimulating hormone (FSH) and luteinizing hormone (LH) are elevated in both older men and women. The change in the female is about threefold that in the male and persists into extreme old age. Secretion rises significantly after a stimulus of luteinizing hormone releasing hormone (LH-RH), but the normal feedback control by the peripheral hormones is impaired.

Vasopressin.—Circulating levels of the antidiuretic hormone vasopressin tend to be higher in old people than in the young, and the response to a standard osmotic challenge is exaggerated. Contributing to the increased circulating levels are lowered rates of hepatic and renal clearance.

ADRENAL CORTEX

There is a slight loss of adrenal weight that begins at about age 50 years and is accompanied by an increase in connective tissue, which replaces parenchymal cells and produces a thickening of the capsule. Pigment accumulates throughout the cortex, and the amount of lipid in the zona fasciculata is reduced. There is also a tendency for the demarcation of the three cortical zones to become more diffuse.

Plasma glucocorticoid levels are similar in young and old persons; both show the same pattern of diurnal variation, with the highest values observed in the early morning and low values in the evening. Glucocorticoid concentration measured in the middle of the night, however, tends to be significantly higher in the old than in the young. The distribution of the glucocorticoids does not change with age, but there is a significant depression of the disposal rate. Since the plasma concentration is not dependent on age, the lower rate of disposal matches a lower rate of secretion. The response of the adrenal cortex to ACTH remains normal in old people, and the pituitary release of ACTH in response to stress is, likewise, intact.

Circulating levels of aldosterone are lower in the old than in the young. Aldosterone secretion is controlled by the renin-angiotensin system, by the plasma potassium concentration, and, to only a small extent in man, by ACTH. In the old, there is a depressed response of the renin-initiated system both to the acute alterations in blood volume distribution (e.g., posture) and to chronic salt and water depletion. The response to ACTH is not affected by age. Secretion of the adrenal androgens decreases with age, but since no clear functional role has been assigned to these hormones, the significance is unknown.

PANCREAS

The weight of the pancreas remains stable throughout adulthood and into old age. Very little is known about age-related alterations in the fine structure because of the extremely rapid autolysis the tissue undergoes.

Insulin.—Resting levels of insulin secretion remain stable with age, but deterioration of glucose tolerance, as demonstrated by the usual tests, begins in middle adulthood and progresses steadily with age. The blood glucose level 2 hours after a 50-g oral dose of glucose increases about 6% for each decade; thus, half of older subjects display a tolerance curve outside the norm plus two standard deviations as opposed to that seen in young adults. Since the prevalence of adult-onset diabetes increases with age, it is difficult to differentiate between physiologic decline and a genetic trait. The questions that arise from the observation of the low glucose tolerance are (1) is there a reduced response of the β-cell to the glucose load, and (2) is there a change in tissue sensitivity to insulin? The application of the glucose clamp technique, in which the plasma glucose concentration is servocontrolled, has led to the conclusion that β-cell sensitivity is indeed decreased in older persons. The intravenous insulin tolerance test of peripheral sensitivity to insulin shows this to be unchanged with age. The possibility also exists that in older people a larger fraction of the immunoreactive insulin is, in fact, the biologically inactive precursor proinsulin. Further, it is important to remember that glucose tolerance is modulated by activity and by obesity so that only a fraction of the observed alteration, if in fact any, may be related to an aging change or genetic trait.

Glucagon.—Information on age-related changes in glucagon secretion is very limited. The fasting plasma level does not change with age, nor is there a reduction in the increase following arginine provocation. One study has shown that the rise in the blood glucose level in response to the administration of exogenous glucagon is both delayed in time and reduced in magnitude.

THYROID

Although significant changes occur in thyroid structure with age—for example, reduced follicular diameter, reduced epithelial cell height, and reduced amount of colloid—thyroid function appears to remain adequate. Although the basal metabolic rate declines steadily with age, this change is not seen when caloric output is standardized to total body water or lean body mass rather than to surface area. There is a slight reduction in the concentration of thyroxine-binding globulin (TBG), but the serum concentration of thyroxine (T_4) remains essentially unchanged. The concentration of triiodothyronine (T_3) diminishes significantly with age, and this has been attributed to a reduced conversion of T_4 to T_3 in extrathyroidal locations. The disposal rate of T_4 is reduced as a consequence of the declining activity of hepatic enzyme systems or a lack of strenuous physical activity, which is a powerful stimulant to disposal. In old men, but not in old women, secretion of the pituitary trophic factor, thyroid-stimulating hormone (TSH), is reduced in response to the hypothalamic releasing factor, thyrotropin releasing hormone (TRH). In both sexes, direct stimulation of thyroid secretion by TSH or by fever shows the responsiveness of the gland to be unchanged with age. The retention of a normal circulating level of T_4 with a reduced rate of disposal suggests that the feedback control system has been readjusted.

PARATHYROID

The major aging structural change in the parathyroid is an increase in the interstitial adipose tissue. The accumulation of fat may account for as much as 40% of the weight of the gland. There is a striking difference between the sexes in the pattern of change in the circulating levels of parahormone with age. In men, the level starts out low and increases until the sixth decade; the circulating level in persons in their 50s is about three times that seen in those in their 20s. After the peak in the 50s, levels decline back toward the values found in young men. Young women, on the other hand, have a circulating level about twice that in young men; the value declines to its lowest in the 40s and then climbs steadily with further aging with no sign of the decrease seen in men. This progressive rise after middle age in women is exaggerated in those who develop postmenopausal osteoporosis. The major route of disposal of the hormone is degradation in the kidney, and in experimental animals, it has been shown that this process slows with age. The changed circulating levels probably reflect the interaction of changes in the rates of both secretion and elimination.

Although these aging changes in the endocrine system are relatively small, the question continues to be raised as to what extent they might be causative rather than consequent. At the moment, one can only speculate as to how far normalization of hormonal factors might retard the aging process.

SUGGESTED READING

Endocrine System

Dolocek R: Endocrine changes in the elderly. *Triangle* 1985; 24:17–33.

Korenman SG (ed): *Endocrine Aspects of Aging.* New York, Elsevier Biomedical, 1982.

Meites J: Changes in neuroendocrine control of anterior pituitary function during aging. *Neuroendocrinology* 1982; 34:151–156.

Noth RH, Mazzaferri EL: Age and the endocrine system. *Clin Geriatr Med* 1985; 1:223–250.

Roth GS, Hess GD: Changes in the mechanisms of hormone and neurotransmitter action during aging. Current status of the role of receptor and postreceptor alterations. A review. *Mech Ageing Dev* 1982; 20:175–194.

9

The Reproductive System

The human female and some subhuman primates differ from other mammals in that cessation of reproductive capability is not contemporaneous with death. Today a woman can expect to live for about 30 years after the menstrual cycle ceases. The cessation of the reproductive function is a dramatic manifestation of aging in a major physiologic system. Associated with the loss of cyclic changes in the levels of the sex hormones, numerous imbalances occur in neural and endocrine regulatory mechanisms, which together form the female climacteric. In men, no episode in aging corresponds to the menopause. Reproductive function shows a slow progressive decline rather than an abrupt termination. As a consequence, men normally have no climacteric, although some metabolic and neuroendocrine imbalances are found in hypogonadic men.

OVARY

From the prenatal period onward, oocytes are lost from the ovary, and by the time of menarche, only 10% of the primordial follicles that were in the fetal ovary remain (Fig 9–1). From the age of 30 years onward, ovarian weight decreases, the quantity of connective tissues increases, and perfusion diminishes. With aging, there is also a reduction in the number of follicles that undergo normal growth and development. Many show maturational defects possibly indicative of a lowered responsiveness of the ovary to the gonadotropin. Before the onset of the menopause, there is a reduced formation of corpora lutea. Since these are essential to the maintenance of pregnancy, women have

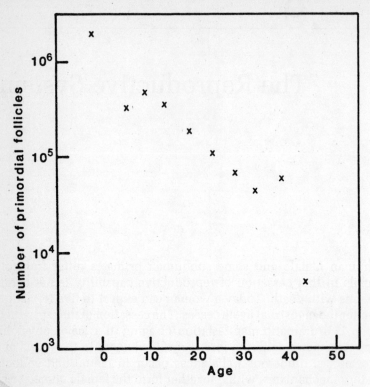

FIG 9–1.
The loss of primordial follicles from the ovary. (Based on data from Beck E: Quantitative morphological investigations of the follicular system in women. *Acta Anat (Basel)* 1952; 14:108.)

lower fertility and higher rates of miscarriage in these years. Ova formed in the later reproductive life have diminished viability and higher rates of chromosomal abnormality.

FEMALE SECONDARY SEX ORGANS

Adequate circulating levels of the sex hormones are essential to the maintenance of the secondary organs. The uterus reaches its peak weight at age 30 years and by age 50 years has lost half of its mass. There is a major loss of both collagen and elastin, and the remaining collagen shows the typical aging changes attributed to the development of cross-linking. The fallopian tubes also shrink. The vagina shrinks, and the wall thins. In the presence of decreased estrogen activity, the vaginal lining is reduced to a single layer of fattened cells, and there may be patches of erosion. Drying and keratinization occur in the vaginal outlet, and the labia and clitoris diminish in size. Loss of pubic hair occurs late in the aging process. In the mammary glands, alveoli are lost, and the size of the ducts decreases as their lining thins. There is often some loss of adipose tissue. This loss of mass, together with the aging changes in the connective tissue, leads to flaccid and drooping breasts. The nipples shrink and lose their ability to become erect.

TESTIS

There is little or no loss of weight of the testis with aging, but there is an increase in the fibrous tissue of the intertubular spaces. The basement membrane around the seminiferous tubules thickens. Of the three cell types of the testis—germinal cells, Sertoli's cells, and the interstitial cells of Leydig—the latter show the greatest change with age. These cells, which are the source of testosterone and androgens, accumulate lipid from puberty to approximately age 30 years. From this time onward, cells are lost, and remaining cells show a decreased lipid content that correlates well with the decline observed in androgen excretion. By contrast, Sertoli's cells continue to accumulate lipid throughout life, and this is suggested to be related to estrogen production. Sperm production continues into advanced old age, but the rate slows, and there is an increase in the proportion of abnormal forms. Active spermatozoa are present in the ejaculates of 70% of men 60 to 70 years of age and in 50% of the ejaculates of men 80 to 90 years old, although in this older group, the sperm count is only 50% of that in the young adult.

MALE SECONDARY SEX ORGANS

Changes begin to appear in the prostate of men from age 40 years onward. First, there are diffuse changes in part of the gland; then smooth muscle atrophies and is replaced by denser connective tissue; the columnar epithelium is converted to cuboidal forms and concretions (corpora amylacea) appear in the ducts. As aging progresses, these changes encompass the whole gland. Acini are lost, and connective tissue continues to accumulate, leading to the common prostatic hypertrophy. The seminal vesicles accumulate granular pigment, some of which finds its way into the semen.

REPRODUCTIVE HORMONES

As maturing follicles are lost from the ovary, estrogen levels fall, precipitately at first and then at a declining rate. Circulating estrogen, which is at a level of about 20% of that seen before menopause, is not of ovarian origin but is derived from the peripheral conversion of androgens by adipose tissue. The ovaries continue to secrete androgen after menopause, and the circulating level is maintained by the ovaries as well as by the adrenal glands.

In the male, a fall in the circulating level of testosterone begins in early adulthood. Reports of the extent of fall are conflicting, probably because of differences in study populations and in sampling methods. Some reports indicate that serum testosterone is in the normal range, although low, even in the 70s and 80s. Most reports agree that the circadian rhythm of testosterone release is depressed in the aged male. The secretion of estrogens by Sertoli's cells of the testis continues, and this maintains some feedback control of the pituitary trophic factors. The response of the testis to stimulation by human chorionic gonadotropin is blunted.

In both male and female, the pituitary gonadotropins rise, although the magnitude of the rise in the male is relatively modest (Fig 9–2). It has been reported that the biologic activity of both follicle-stimulating hormone (FSH) and luteinizing hormone (LH) in the postmenopausal female is increased over its previous value. The hypothalamic releasing system for the gonadotropins appears to be relatively intact although hypothalamic content of luteinizing hormone releasing hormone (LH-RH) is reduced after menopause. In the experimental animal, pituitary sensitivity to LH-RH has been demonstrated to increase, but it is not known whether this phenomenon also occurs in the human female.

THE CLIMACTERIC

Although the climacteric is not a universal phenomenon, most women experience a complex of symptoms in the years immediately following the menopause. These symptoms of the "change of life" include vasomotor instability marked by "hot flashes" most commonly in the dermatomes of the cervical segments, outbursts of sweating, paroxysmal tachycardia, and chills. Emotional changes, bouts of depression, and withdrawal from family also occur but less frequently. The postmenopausal period is also marked by an imbalance in osteoclastic and osteoblastic activity, which leads to a large incidence of osteoporosis. Although not confined to women, the extent of this loss of bone mineral is much less in men. The menopause also leads to changes in the secretion pattern of growth hormone; the morning peak is lost. Since the climacteric is almost uniquely a human menopause, no animal model exists for investigation of the syndrome. However, evidence from rats has led to a proposal that the link between estrogen deficiency and the postmenopausal syndrome might be provided by some neurotransmitters that can be modulated in activity by the ovarian

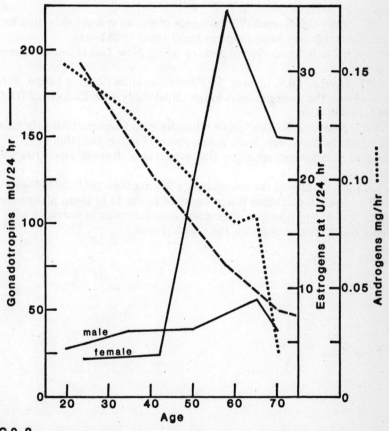

FIG 9–2.
Changes in the excretion of gonadotropins, estrogens, and androgens with age. mU = milliunits. (Based on data from Pincus G, et al: The excretion of urinary steroids by men and women of various ages. *J Gerontol* 1954; 9:113, and Johnsen SG: A clinical routine method for the quantitative determination of gonadotrophins in 24-hour urine samples: II. Normal values for men and women at all age groups from puberty to senescence. *Acta Endocrinol (Copenh)* 1959; 31:209.

steroids. Such modulation has been demonstrated for the catecholamines and the prostaglandins. The postmenopausal symptoms last for
only months, or in the extreme case, for a few years. Presumably, this
termination of the syndrome is brought about by other non–estrogen-
modulated changes in neurotransmitter synthesis and the disposal that
occurs as aging progresses.

SUGGESTED READING

Reproductive System

Johnson L, Petty CS, Neaves WB: Influence of age on sperm production and
testicular weights in men. *J Reprod Fertil* 1984; 70:211–218.

Korenman SG (ed): *Endocrine Aspects of Aging.* New York, Elsevier Biomedical, 1982.

Metcalf MG, Donald RA, Livesey JH: Pituitary-ovarian function before, during and after the menopause: A longitudinal study. *Clin Endocrinol (Oxf)*
1982; 17:489–494.

Rakoff AE, Nowroozi K: The female climacteric, in Greenblatt RB (ed): *Geriatric Endocrinology.* New York, Raven Press, 1978, pp 165–190.

Vermeulen A: Androgen secretion after age 50 in both sexes. *Horm Res* 1983;
18:37–42.

Yen SSC: The biology of the menopause. *J Reprod Med* 1977; 18:387–396.

Zumoff B, Strain GW, Dream J: Age variation in the 24-hr mean plasma concentrations of androgens, estrogens and gonadotropins in normal adult
men. *J Clin Endocrinol Metab* 1982; 54:534–538.

10

Aging of Regulatory Mechanisms

Among the theories of aging that were previously mentioned was that of impairment of the body's homeostatic regulatory system. Our examination of the organ systems has shown limitations of function that are often due to changes in the effector tissues. In other instances, function appears to be impaired by inadequate input of information from receptor systems. The central elements of regulation are also susceptible to age-related changes. Among these elements are the autonomic nervous system and its higher centers together with the endocrine system and the neurotransmitter substances. The latter have already been considered. In addition, it is important to remember that many homeostatic processes require the participation of conscious behavior. (It's not enough to be "waterproof"; we also need to know to "come in out of the rain.")

AUTONOMIC NERVOUS SYSTEM

Despite its name, this division of the nervous system is not autonomous but rather provides the efferent limb for regulatory reflexes. It shares with the somatic nervous system impairments with aging that occur at the level of receptors, in nerve transmission, in the integrating centers, in the ganglia, and at the interface with effector systems.

The receptor elements of these loops, in general, show a loss of sensitivity and require greater levels or greater duration of stimulation for a response to be elicited. The regulatory centers, many of which can be identified with hypothalamic nuclei or more diffuse collections of neurons in the brain stem, are not, as a general rule, subject to a major aging loss of neuron number. Rather they show a loss of precision in the sense that greater deviations from the target value are necessary before corrective action is initiated. The setting or target values appear to be only minimally affected by age.

Information on the aging of the human autonomic outflow system is fragmentary at best, but animal studies have demonstrated changes in all stages of information flow. These studies have shown that with age, greater intensities of stimulation must be applied to sympathetic or parasympathetic nerves to elicit a change in the end organ. At the autonomic ganglia, sensitivity to preganglionic stimulation is lost, and there is a reduction in the maximum frequency with which impulses can be transmitted through the ganglionic synapses. At the same time, end organs and ganglia show an increased sensitivity to neurotransmitters applied directly. This phenomenon is clearly related to "denervation hypersensitivity." With aging, there is a reduction in the number of nervous system elements and reduced neurotransmitter synthesis. In the cholinergic parts of the system—the ganglia and the muscarinic terminations—the reduced rate of synthesis is accompanied by a decreased concentration of acetylcholinesterase. The effect of this is to protect the function of the end organ. The balance between reduced synthesis and reduced disposal differs from organ to organ so that hypersensitivity is a variable phenomenon. Old ganglia also have an increased sensitivity to blocking agents such as hexamethonium. In the adrenergic system, on the other hand, the postsynaptic elements show a reduced sensitivity to excitatory and blocking agents.

In humans, the resting circulating level of norepinephrine is elevated in older subjects, and there is a greater elevation in response to stress. There is no age-related change in levels of epinephrine. The adrenergic agonist, isoproterenol produces less vasodilation in the vessels of the old than in the young, but the response to nitrite or nitroprusside is not affected. One possibility is that receptor density changes with age although there is no direct quantitative evidence for this. The smooth muscle of the aortic media of old animals contracts less in response to norepinephrine. Although this again may suggest a reduced receptor density, it may equally well result from an increased stiffness of the tunica media of the vessel as the content of connective tissue increases.

Other aspects of changed regulation of the cardiovascular system were mentioned in Chapter 5 and many of these can be attributed to changed sensitivity of the baroreceptor system. In many old people, this produces significant orthostatic hypotension, since neither the peripheral resistance nor the heart rate responds adequately to the challenge of venous pooling that occurs on standing. In some old persons, the cardiovascular regulatory system may not be able to maintain the arterial pressure when muscle vasculature is dilated by exercise or by the administration of nitroprusside. Performance of the Valsalva maneuver by old persons produces a greater decrease in pressure during the straining phase than in a young adult, and on release of the intrathoracic pressure, there is no rebound to the elevated pressure. Fainting as a consequence of coughing or straining to urinate is a reflection of this same impaired regulation.

A rather general aging effect on the homeostatic regulatory system is an increased time required for equilibration to occur, even at the level of exchanges between tissues and their environment of interstitial fluid. As a consequence, the response time of the system is extended and the valuable characteristic of prompt correction of disturbance compromised. Some principles discussed here are illustrated in considering the regulation of specific aspects of the internal environment.

BODY TEMPERATURE

The body temperature is a reflection of the heat balance of the body—the balance between heat gain and heat loss. Temperatures measured in various parts of the body differ reflecting different rates of heat gain and loss. We speak of the "core" temperature—the average temperature of the deep tissues—and distinguish this from the surface or skin temperature. The latter varies with site of measurement, being higher on the trunk than on more peripheral sites. The temperature of the skin reflects the local balance of heat delivery by blood reaching the surface and the rate of dissipation of the heat to the environment. Our sense of thermal comfort is derived from the heat balance at the body surface, and most adults have a comfort zone centered around an average skin temperature of 33°C. This comfort zone shifts a little with age.

Regulation of the body temperature (that is, the heat content) resides in the hypothalamus where two centers can be identified: (1) a center situated in the preoptic area, which, on stimulation, activates mechanisms of heat dissipation; and (2) a posterior hypothalamic area, which largely controls heat generation and heat conservation. The setting of the body's thermostat, or in other words, the target temperature for the regulation, is controlled from the posterior hypothalamus, which is acted on by the ascending arousal outflow from the brain stem reticular formation.

The centers act on information from two sources, (1) the temperature of the blood perfusing the hypothalamus, and (2) the cutaneous thermoreceptors. Information from these sources is weighted so that a unit change in blood temperature is about ten times as effective as a unit change in skin temperature.

Core temperatures are commonly measured in the mouth or rectum, but a superior reflection of the central temperature is obtained in the insulated auditory meatus (the tympanic temperature). This site is not convenient for routine use, and an almost equally reliable measurement can be made in a freshly voided urine sample.

Homeothermy, the state of constant body temperature, is maintained by balancing heat gain with heat loss. Table 10–1 lists the factors involved in the mechanism of gain, conservation, and loss, many of which are changed with age.

In the area of metabolic heat gain, the old person is at a disadvantage because of the lesser muscle mass that provides a reduced basal heat production. This disadvantage extends to heat generation by voluntary activity or shivering. As part of the aging of the skin, thinning of the epidermis and subcutaneous fat occurs, thus reducing natural insulation. Skin blood flow is reduced pari passu with the fall in cardiac output, and the hands and feet especially are cold. The use of clothing to increase surface insulation requires an awareness of the need as well as the physical capability to don extra layers. Perception of this need is often blunted in older individuals.

When the need is for the dissipation of heat, the impairment of the skin circulation is a considerable disadvantage since the physical routes of heat loss call for an increased surface temperature. There is a considerable reduction in the density of sweat glands as the skin ages so that there is a quantitative loss of this most effective avenue of heat loss. Thinning of the skin and the small increase in tidal volume shown by the elderly increase the insensible loss of water by evaporation, but this does not contribute a very significant amount to the heat balance.

THERMAL SENSITIVITY IN THE ELDERLY

It is often held that old people prefer environments that are warmer than those that are comfortable to younger people, but there is very little direct evidence to support this. In fact, some studies of subjective comfort have shown that old persons are inclined to describe as "slightly

TABLE 10–1.
Mechanisms of Thermoregulation*

Basic Mechanisms	Factors Involved
Heat gain	
Metabolic	Basal metabolic activity[†]
	Voluntary muscle activity[†]
	Muscle tone[†]
	Involuntary muscle activity, e.g., shivering[†]
Physical, when skin temperature lower than ambient temperature	Warming of body surface by physical means
	Conduction from warm objects
	Radiation from warm surroundings (or sun)
	Convection from passage of warm air over body
Heat conservation	
Insulation	Peripheral insulation afforded by skin and subcutaneous tissue[†]
	Reduction of heat delivery to skin circulation[†]
	Clothing
Heat dissipation	
Physical, when skin temperature higher than ambient temperature	Radiation from warmer skin to cool surroundings
	Conduction by contact with cool objects
	Convection by passage of cool air over body surface
	All dependent on increasing heat delivery to surface circulation[†]
Physical, by evaporative means	Evaporation of water from upper respiratory tract[†]
	Diffusional loss of water through skin[†]
	Sweating, requiring neural activation of sweat glands

*From Kenney RA: Physiology of aging. *Clin Geriatr Med* 1985; 1:37–59. Used by permission.
†Changed by aging.

warm" conditions that in fact are producing a net heat loss from the body. Such a lowered sensitivity means, as already mentioned, that the old persons is less likely, even if capable, to take the appropriate action to conserve heat or produce more heat. Old people often report as "too warm" conditions that the young find comfortable.

As we saw earlier, the efficiency of the central elements of a control system can be judged by how quickly corrective actions can be initiated. When exposed to cold, old people begin to shiver later than do the young, although once shivering is initiated, there is an effective increase in heat production. Likewise, when exposed to a heat load, the old person shows a delayed sweating response, and once sweating is established, it continues for a longer time since the rate of sweating is low, and the heat load, therefore, persists longer.

When a person is at rest in a comfortable environment, there is no difference in body temperature between young and old, a fact which demonstrates that the target temperature is not age dependent. The problem lies in the sensitivity of the control that has to receive a large error signal before the response begins.

All of the changes that have been described expose old people to the hazard of thermal injury. The frequency of death from hyperthermia increases rapidly after the age of 60 years. The effects of high heat loads are cumulative, and the incidence of hyperthermia increases steadily as a spell of hot weather continues. This progressive morbidity is probably due to the failure to maintain water and salt balance. The increased demand on the circulation in heat calls for good vascular filling, and sweating requires the availability of large volumes of fluid. The older person may be insensible to the need or be incapable of acquiring the necessary fluid. The course of hyperthermia, once initiated, can be rapid. When the body temperature reaches 41°C, the central control mechanisms become depressed. At this point, the chemical reactions of metabolism become driven at an increasing rate so that a positive feedback situation develops. In this phase, the body temperature rises rapidly and death, usually from respiratory depression, ensues when it reaches 44°C.

Reduced cutaneous sensibility to cold, the inability to generate sufficient metabolic heat, poor inherent insulation, and reduced capability to microclimatize by way of clothing or other adjustment of the environment all serve to make cold a particular hazard to old people. It is only fairly recently that the magnitude and significance of this problem has been appreciated. Studies undertaken in England have suggested that 10% of the older population may be susceptible to "accidental hypothermia." The criterion for hypothermia was established as a temperature of less than 35°C measured in a sample of freshly voided urine. On this basis, more than 3% of older individuals admitted to hospitals (for causes other than hypothermia) were judged to be hypothermic. In this country, a survey suggested that 25,000 people may have suffered a bout of hypothermia in 1975; the figure would almost certainly be higher today. The afflicted individual not uncommonly is an old person living alone in housing that is less than ideal. Unheated bedrooms and bathrooms are very common, precipitating environments for the condition, but the occurrence of hypothermia is not confined to those living without adequate domestic heating.

Low metabolism and inadequate heat conservation allow the core temperature to fall toward a critical value of 34°C. At this point, central regulation becomes impaired, and a fall in rate of metabolism establishes a positive feedback loop. As the temperature continues to fall, a sinus bradycardia becomes intense and myocardial metabolism critically depressed. Arrhythmias supervene, leading to death by ventricular fibrillation. In addition to the metabolic factors that have been mentioned, alcohol and antidepressant drugs can be additional causative factors, but economic considerations expressed in inadequate diet and inadequate domestic heating are major culprits. One of every three persons whose temperatures fall to 32°C will die; those who experience severe levels of hypothermia (that is, a body temperature of 28°C) have a mortality rate of 75%.

An additional life-threatening component of inadequate thermal defense against cooling is the "cold-kidney," which loses its ability to conserve water. The consequent diuresis, coupled in all likelihood with an inadequate fluid intake, can rapidly depress vascular filling to a critical level.

ACID-BASE REGULATION

The pH of the body fluids is only mildly affected by age, and the differences between young and old are seen only when the acid-base balance is challenged. A normal, nonvegetarian diet imposes a net load of acid amounting to 50 to 100 mEq/day in addition to approximately 700 mEq of carbonic acid in the form of carbon dioxide. The nonvolatile acid load derives from the oxidation of sulfur and phosphorus of protein and phosphorus of the phospholipids.

Three processes are fundamental to acid-base regulation: (1) buffering of the load of acid or base, (2) adjustment of the pH toward normal by respiratory modifications, and (3) renal elimination of the excess acid or base.

Buffering of a load of noncarbonic acid is initially rapid, using bicarbonate of plasma and interstitial fluid, then slower using the proton-acceptor capacity of intracellular protein, and still slower using the buffering power of the bone. The total buffer capacity of the old person is less than that of the young. The interstitial fluid volume per unit of body weight is lower, and the bicarbonate concentration is lower. The reduced lean tissue mass and the loss of bone mineral both reduce the available tissue buffering.

The rapid phase of buffering of a strong acid produces carbonic acid, which can readily be eliminated by the lungs. Although the old person has diminished respiratory reserve and some reduction of diffusing capacity at the alveolar membrane, the effect on carbon dioxide elimination is negligible. The high solubility of carbon dioxide and the consequent high diffusibility provide a wide safety margin. Only when a gross challenge calls for an extreme ventilatory response is an age-related deficiency seen.

The third stage of regulation, which restores the buffer systems to their normal state, is performed by the kidney. In a young person, this correction requires hours or even days. The role of the kidney is three-fold. First, it regulates the quantity of bicarbonate that is reabsorbed or allowed to escape into the urine. The response to an acid load is to maximize this recovery. Second, the kidney eliminates hydrogen ion by way of the buffers presented to the distal tubule. Third, the kidney regenerates buffer base by replacing the urinary cation with the ammonium ion.

The reduced effective mass of the kidney clearly hinders all three functions. A reduced rate of formation of glomerular filtrate leads to a reduced presentation of bicarbonate to the proximal tubule. In the case of an acid load, this is not important since the object is to maximize the recovery of bicarbonate. On the other hand, if the disturbance of the acid-base balance calls for the elimination of excess bicarbonate, the process is necessarily slow since only the amount filtered per unit time can be excreted.

The low glomerular filtration rate leads to a reduced delivery of buffers to the distal nephron where the titratable acidity of the urine is generated. Since only a limited gradient of pH can be generated, a reduction in the total quantity of the buffer limits the elimination of hydrogen ions. Some compensation for the lower glomerular filtration of buffers is afforded by the decreased reabsorption of phosphate in the old kidney. The magnitude of this change is trivial in relation to the net result, however.

The old kidney has a reduced ability to deaminate glutamine to provide "new" urinary cations. The ammonia that enters the distal tubule fluid also serves to trap hydrogen ions, which are then excreted in urine. When the acid-base regulation is tested by the administration of oral ammonium chloride, the rate of elimination of the resulting load of hydrochloric acid in the old person is only one third of that in the young adult (see summary Table 10–2).

VOLUME AND TONICITY OF THE BODY FLUIDS

Homeostasis of the volume and tonicity of the body fluids is accomplished by a precise regulation of the water and salt content of the extracellular compartment (Table 10–3). The intracellular compartment has a rather passive role; its volume is controlled by the osmotic pressure of the interstitial fluid and its solute content defended by specific transport mechanisms of the cell membrane. Although the membrane system that excludes the sodium ion and retains potassium in the cell shows some loss of efficiency in the old red cell, the cells of an old person generally retain their ion selectivity, and the equilibrium between intracellular and extracellular compartments is maintained.

When a person has free access to fluid and is eating an adequate diet, the intake of water and salt is well in excess of minimal requirements. In the older person, the minimal requirement of water is somewhat increased by an increase in the percutaneous loss as a consequence of thinning of the skin and a potential extra loss via the kidney as a consequence of reduced concentrating ability. The kidney is the effector system controlling the body's content of water and salt, and essential to this system are the controls exercised by vasopressin and aldosterone.

Circulating levels of vasopressin tend to be higher in the old than in the young, and this is probably the result of a slowing of disposal of the peptide by hepatic metabolism and renal excretion. The responsiveness of the hypothalamus to the osmotic and volume signals that

TABLE 10–2.
Acid-Base Regulatory System*

Mechanism	Factors Involved
Buffering	
Bicarbonate system	Extracellular fluid volume[†]
	Buffer base concentration[†]
Intracellular protein	Cell mass[†]
Bone	Mineral content of bone[†]
Respiratory adjustment	
Elimination of CO_2	Chemoreceptor responsiveness to arterial Pco_2[†]
Retention of CO_2	Alveolar ventilation[†]
Renal adjustment	
Proximal segment	Bicarbonate filtration[†]
	Intracellular and luminal carbonic anhydrase
	Bicarbonate reabsorption
Distal segments	Intracellular carbonic anhydrase
	Competition with K^+ for secretory gradient
	Supply of buffers for generation of titratable acidity[†]
	Cellular glutaminase for generation of NH_4^+

*From Kenney RA: Physiology of aging. *Clin Geriatr Med* 1985; 1:37–59. Used by permission.
[†]Changed by aging.

TABLE 10–3.

Fluid Volume and Tonicity Regulation*

Mechanism	Factors Involved
Salt and water acquisition	Thirst and access to water[t]
	Adequate dietary salt
	Ingestion and absorption
Nonregulatory losses	
Respiratory evaporation	Alveolar ventilation[t]
Insensible sweating	Cutaneous permeability[t]
	Environmental humidity
Bowel	Vomiting
	Diarrhea
Kidney	Minimal urine volume[t]
Regulated Renal Excretion	
Water conservation (urinary concentration)	Adequate circulating levels of vasopressin
	Renal responsiveness to vasopressin[t]
	Medullary osmotic stratification[t]
Water elimination (urinary)	Glomerular filtration[t]
	Selective solute absorption[t]
Salt conservation	Adequate circulating levels of aldosterone[t]
	Intact tubular reabsorptive mechanisms[t]
Salt elimination	Glomerular filtration[t]
	Regulated tubular reabsorption[t]
	Diuretics
	Adequate urine volume

*From Kenney RA: Physiology of aging. *Clin Geriatr Med* 1985; 1:37–59. Used by permission.
[t]Changed by aging.

regulate vasopressin neurosecretion appears to be increased by age as does the release of hormone from the posterior pituitary.

Circulating levels of aldosterone are lower in the old person, and the responsiveness of the zona glomerulosa to both the local signal of the sodium-to-potassium ratio in the plasma and the more effective secretory signal from the renin-angiotensin system is reduced. Basic to overall regulation of the body fluids is the provision of adequate volumes of glomerular filtrate on which the endocrine-governed tubular processes can operate. When the rates of glomerular filtration are lower, the absolute quantities of water or salt that can be eliminated or conserved per unit of time are reduced, even when the tubular processes retain their efficiency. However, the efficiency of the tubular processes is not retained, especially in regard to water. The medulla of the old kidney has less osmotic stratification, and furthermore, the distal tubules and collecting ducts become less responsive to vasopressin. Vasopressin action at these sites involve cyclic adenosine monophosphate (cAMP) as the second messenger, and this may be an example of a general reduced activity of adenyl cyclase in aging. Although in the young adult, maximal water conservation can lead to the production of urine that is four times as concentrated as plasma, in the old, this ratio falls to less than three. The elimination of solute loads in the old is thus expensive in terms of absolute volumes of water lost and slow because of the low filtration. When the challenge is to eliminate excess water, the deficiency of the old kidney is seen in the diluting operation. In the young person, urine can be formed that is less than one tenth as concentrated as plasma. Impaired salt recovery in the old kidney shifts the minimal osmotic concentration of urine closer to that of plasma. Excretion of water load is thus slow (low glomerular filtration) and expensive of salt. Given adequate time to restore balance, the old person performs adequately, but the slow rates of elimination or conservation tend to produce larger, longer-sustained shifts from the target position.

Although the intake of water and salt normally exceeds minimal requirements, intake usually involves a voluntary response to the sensations of thirst in the old and appetite. There is no evidence that the primary sensation of thirst in the old is lessened, but they may have physical problems in obtaining and drinking fluids. The acuity of taste for salt is reduced in the old; thus they tend to increase their salt intake in an effort to satisfy their taste. The danger for old people is thus dehydration and hyperosmolarity rather than salt depletion and hypoosmolarity. It is especially important to bear in mind the poorer regulation of volume and tonicity in the older person when fluids are administered parenterally or when diuretics, which may severely challenge the water and solute balance of the body, are prescribed.

SUGGESTED READING

Collins KJ: *Hypothermia: The Facts.* New York, Oxford University Press, 1983.

Collins KJ, Exton-Smith AN, James MH, et al: Functional changes in autonomic nervous responses with aging. *Age Aging* 1980; 9:17–24.

Davis BB, Zenser TV: Biological changes in thermoregulation in the elderly, in Davis BB, Wood WG (eds): *Homeostatic Function and Aging.* New York, Raven Press, 1985.

Fox RH, MacGibbon R, Davies L, et al: Problems of the old and the cold. *Br Med J* 1973; 1:21–24.

Frolkis VV: Regulatory processes in the mechanism of aging. *Exp Gerontol* 1968; 3:113–123.

Lybarger JA, Kilbourne EM: Hyperthermia and hypothermia in the elderly, in Davis BB, Wood WG (eds): *Homeostatic Function and Aging.* New York, Raven Press, 1985.

McDermott DJ, Tristan FE, Porth CJM, et al: Age-related changes in cardio-vascular responses to diverse circulatory stresses, in Sleight P (ed), *Arterial Baroceptors and Hypertension*. New York, Oxford University Press, 1981, pp 361–364.

Minnaker K, Rowe J, Sparrow D: Impaired cardiovascular adaptation to vaso-dilation in the elderly. *Gerontologist* 1981; 20:163.

Rowe JW, Troens BR: Sympathetic nervous system and aging in man. *Endocr Rev* 1980; 1:167–179.

PART THREE

Other Consequences of Aging

11

Aging Changes in Higher Functions

Nowhere is it more difficult than in the brain to separate the eugeric changes of normal aging from disease processes. The changes that are regarded as part of normal aging—for example, loss of neurons, alterations in the metabolism of neurotransmitters, and the development of plaques and neurofibrillary inclusions—differ only in a quantitative way from the signs of brain disease. Likewise, the changes in cortical function that are regarded as eugeric may well be part of a continuum that has dementia as its extreme. If this concept is valid, then the reduction of intellectual function displayed by some old people and presently regarded as normal may in fact be either prevented or delayed once we have a sufficient understanding of the interplay of genetic, cardiovascular, and environmental factors in the cause of brain disease.

THE EEG IN THE AGING PERSON

Major alterations occur in the electric activity of the cortex as a consequence of cerebral atrophy or vascular disease. It is therefore difficult to identify alterations that may properly be described as normal aging. It is generally agreed, however, that a slowing of the α-rhythm is typical of the healthy older person. In the young person, the rhythm has a dominant frequency of approximately 10 Hz; in older persons, there is a downward shift to the range of 8 to 9.5 Hz. Within this lower range, the lowest values are seen in the oldest persons. One study has shown that in two age-matched groups, one of "good learners" and one of "poor learners," the latter showed a lower dominant frequency. During middle age, there is an increase in fast activity in the 12-to-30-Hz frequency, and this diminishes with aging. The loss is marked in individuals who have significant mental deterioration. The continued presence of fast activity in the older person is regarded as a good sign. There is increased slow activity of the δ- and θ- frequencies, which, in the normal person, tends to be focal rather than diffuse. The temporal area is a favored site for this activity, but there is no known clinical correlate of this change. Measures of learning, memory, and intelligence quotient (IQ) do not differ between groups that show or do not show this activity. When studied longitudinally, subjects who showed foci of slow activity had more loss of verbal function. Diffuse slow activity involving large cortical areas is associated with severe mental impairment.

AVERAGED EVOKED POTENTIALS

Averaged evoked potentials (AEPs) are potentials recorded from the scalp following the presentation of a stimulus—visual, auditory, or tactile. The potentials are evoked by a series of stimuli presented 1 or 2 seconds apart and are averaged by computer. In this process of averaging, the potentials that are time-locked to the presentation of the stimulus are enhanced and the "noise" or non–time-locked activity diminishes. Records take the form of a series of negative and positive deflections during the 500 or 600 msec following the stimulus. The early events of the evoked response are usually taken to reflect the transmission of information within the nervous system, whereas those that occur later are generally related to processing and storage. Records are analyzed in terms of both the latency (time from the stimulus presentation) of a particular positive or negative wave and the amplitude. When the responses of old and young subjects are compared, differences are seen in both features. Latencies of early waveforms are increased, and there is also an increase in amplitude. These differences occur whether the stimulus is visual or tactile. When individuals with chronic brain syndromes are compared with age-matched controls, the major change is in the later events of the AEP, where latencies are increased and the waveforms attenuated. Similar changes are seen in delirium and during sleep.

The increased latency in healthy old persons could arise from a slowing of the transmission in peripheral elements. If this were the case, then one might expect the stimulus to be dispersed in time. (Com-

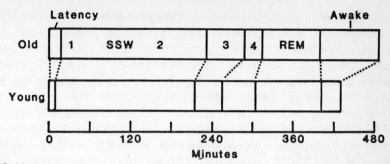

FIG 11–1.
The fractions of time in bed for young and old persons. Numbers refer to the phases of slow-wave sleep (*SSW*). REM = rapid eye movement. (Based on data from Feinberg I, in Terry RD, Gershon S [eds]: *Neurobiology of Aging.* New York, Raven Press, 1976, pp 23–41.)

pare this with the dispersion seen in the electromyogram (EMG) of old subjects, where polyphasic potentials are common.) One would expect the amplitudes of the waveforms to be reduced. Since amplitudes typically increase, the difference between young and old probably resides centrally. When we consider that age is associated with a reduction in the numbers of cortical neurons, the explanation of the phenomenon may be that in the aged there is greater synchrony of discharge of the neurons, perhaps resulting from fewer competing channels of information. An alternative explanation may be that in the aged cortex there is less inhibitory input. The changed latencies may be a direct reflection of impaired membrane processes of depolarization and repolarization.

SLEEP

Sleep studies of young and elderly persons have revealed the following:

1. Older persons take longer to fall asleep than do the young.
2. Total time spent asleep is not different between the groups.
3. Old persons awaken more frequently during the night and spend a longer time awake on each occasion. The older person thus spends longer total time in bed (Fig 11–1).
4. The transition between sleep and wakefulness is abrupt in old people in contrast with the period of "coming to the surface" that young people go through. Old people are thus considered "light sleepers."

The pattern of sleep is conveniently described in terms of the electroencephalographic (EEG) pattern and the presence or absence of rapid eye movements. Sleep is thus divided into slow-wave sleep (SSW) and sleep accompanied by rapid eye movements (SREM). Slow-wave sleep can be divided into stages on the basis of the dominant EEG pattern. The transition from the waking stage to sleep is marked by the appearance of irregular fast activity of low amplitude. This is stage 1 of slow-wave sleep and is usually of short duration. Stage 2 is characterized by low-amplitude, slow wave forms. "Sleep spindles" may appear in which the amplitude waxes and wanes. Stage 3 typically shows the features of stage 2 with the addition of high-voltage δ-rhythm occupying half or less of the period under study. Stage 4 is dominated by high-voltage δ-activity. This is the deepest sleep in terms of the level of stimulus needed for arousal. It is most common in the early part of sleep and occurs less frequently as the night progresses. An association has been suggested between stage 4 SSW and the "metabolic repair" of the waking period. The EEG during SREM is typically irregular and of low voltage; there are no sleep spindles. In the elderly, the time occupied by stage 4 sleep is about half of the young value, but there is a compensatory increase in the amount of stage 3 sleep. It appears that in the elderly, the high-voltage δ-activity that is the criterion for these stages becomes more diffusely distributed among lower-amplitude activity. In both young and old persons, the sum of the durations of both 3 and 4 remains close to 20% of the sleeping time. However the reduction in stage 4 SSW correlates with the reduction in the bursts of secretion of growth hormone that principally occur in this phase.

Sleep spindles occur less frequently in the old, and they are of a lower frequency and amplitude. A similar depression of spindle activity is seen in young hypothyroid individuals. In these cases, adequate replacement therapy normalizes the pattern.

Sleep accompanied by REM shows only a slight reduction with age, but the pattern of appearance of this phase changes. In young people, the early bouts of SREM are short, and they lengthen progressively during the night. In the old, the first bout of SREM is significantly longer than subsequent ones.

No correlation has been made between sleep pattern and brain function, although hypotheses have been offered. One, for example, proposes that the phases of sleep reflect stages in the metabolic activity of the brain that are essentially complementary to the waking information-processing functions.

DREAMING

When a young person is awakened during a period of SREM, dreams can regularly be recalled; dreaming is rare in the person who wakes during SSW. This observation has led to the identification of SREM as "dreaming sleep." The time in which dreams can be recalled is limited. If awakening is delayed more than a few minutes after the end of SREM, no recall is possible. This suggests that waking at the end of SREM is necessary for consolidation of the memory. The major change that occurs with aging is a sharp reduction in dream recall even when the person is awakened immediately after SREM. One study of dream content has suggested that the old dreamer plays a more passive role than the young.

Penile erections are also temporally related to periods of SREM. In young men, erections accompany about 80% of the periods of SREM. In old men, although there is considerable individual variation, the average frequency of erection is only half that seen in the young. The erections of older men are also less complete.

COGNITIVE FUNCTIONS

In Chapter 7, the effects of aging on sensation have been considered. The processing of this flow of information comprises the cognitive functions that determine which elements of the incoming information should receive attention, what should be discarded, what should be remembered, and finally how this information should guide interaction with the environment. Aging indeed does result in changes in cognitive function, and one may postulate two basic factors in this impairment: (1) a reduction in the quantity of circuitry available in the nervous system (e.g., loss of neurons and loss of synapses) and (2) a reduction in the speed with which processes are carried out. Perception, the extraction of meaning from sensation, is essentially a comparator function involving prior information stored in memory. The outcome of this comparison is a "decision" in terms of the significance of the information that guides its subsequent handling. Changes in perception therefore may result from interference with sensation or with memory.

Attention

Critical to effective everyday functioning is the identification of significant events in the environment, which involves vigilance, selective attention, divided attention, and, as a corollary, selective rejection. These elements of attention can be studied separately by appropriate experiments. The simplest vigilance task often takes the form of watching a dial and observing movement of a needle across its face, the object being to detect all the movements that are arranged to occur randomly. In tests of this kind, old subjects perform as well as young, except when the test is prolonged so that the aging effect at this level appears to be one of easier fatigability. When the task is made more complicated by calling for memory of, for example, a specific sequence of movements, the older subject's performance falls off markedly.

Tests of selective attention insert the relevant stimulus among irrelevant information that serves as distraction. Skill at such a task requires prompt rejection of the irrelevant. There is an age-related impairment that becomes greater as the quantity of the irrelevant information increases. One explanation that has been offered is that, in older subjects, the slower speed of processing increases the time required to identify the irrelevant components of the information flow so that they might be rejected.

Everyday life frequently requires attention to be divided between two sources of information, for example, driving safely through traffic while taking part in a conversation. An aging deficit appears if either target of the attention is made more demanding, dense traffic on a highway or an intense discussion of a complex topic.

Memory and Learning

The stereotype of the aged person is one who is slow to learn, has a poor short-term memory, but has good recall for remote events, i.e., long-term memory. Memory and learning are difficult to separate. Learning may be defined as an alteration in behavior as a result of experience, whereas memory involves the recall of experience or recognition. Since one remembers what is learned, these two functions are probably facets of the same process. The division of memory into two parts, one for recent events and one for more remote, arises from the way in which memory is tested and from the present models of memory formation. One such model is shown in Figure 11–2.

Essentially sensory information is taken into storage, sometimes referred to as "immediate memory," where it is held briefly before being passed to short-term memory. A further process then abstracts the information to form a permanent trace, or engram, that is laid down in long-term memory. At each step in this process relevance is examined and the irrelevant discarded. Information from immediate, short-term, or long-term storage can be brought into "working memory" where action decisions can be initiated. Some descriptions of long-term memory divide this into two parts, generic and episodic. Generic memory is the basic fabric of experience—how to tie one's shoes, the layout of one's neighborhood, the fact that two times two is four—and represents that which has been "learned." Episodic memory differs in that, in this case, information is associated with the context of its acquisition.

Evidence from animal experiments has suggested two fundamental processes in memory, one a facilitation at cholinergic synapses and one involving synthesis of memory-specific peptides. The first is proposed as the mechanism of short-term memory and the second of long-term memory. As has already been mentioned, major age-related changes occur in cholinergic neurotransmission and disposal, and likewise there appears to occur some impairment of protein synthesis with aging.

Short-term memory is often tested by a person's ability to repeat a list of digits read aloud or presented visually. The repetition may be either immediate or delayed for seconds or minutes. Such tests show no aging effect into middle age, and thereafter they show a small but significant decline in results. When recall is delayed, the difference between old and young becomes greater. Another test, this one of recognition memory, involves the presentation of a list of words. The list is then taken away, and the subject is asked to recognize the words in a second longer list. This test reveals a decline beginning in the thirties and reaching a plateau in the sixties and seventies. When long-term memory is tested by recall of historical events, men perform better than women. Information that has a high personal impact is better recalled than neural information.

The latter observations presumably reflect the efficiency of episodic

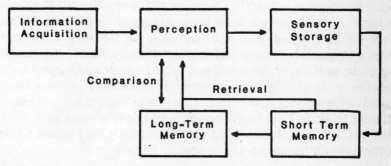

FIG 11–2.
A model for the processing of information into memory.

memory. There is no evidence to support the notion that long-term memory improves the longer the memory is held.

The learning function is often tested by the association of word pairs. The task is learning the "response" word to match a "stimulus" word. There is little difference between old and young persons provided the pacing of learning is slow. If the association is tested in reverse, however, that is the subject is asked to provide the stimulus word when presented with the response, old subjects perform poorly. This is interpreted as showing an impairment of peripheral learning, that is, learning what is an incidental rather than a primary task. One often hears that old people tend to become "single-minded" at a task and ignore what is going on about them. This comment is often pejorative. In a young person, this behavior would be called "concentration." However, these anecdotes are at odds with the observations that suggest increased distractability in the old, and the explanation probably lies in the impairment of a primary sensory pathway.

Research is being done on improving memory function in the old via the restoration of adequate concentrations of acetylcholine in the brain. One line of this work promotes the increased intake of choline in the form of lecithin. An interesting recent observation is that short-term memory can be improved by the intranasal administration of arginine-vasopressin, the antidiuretic hormone. Improvements of memory are also reported following the administration of drugs active on the cerebral vasculature.

Another higher function that is often tested is psychomotor speed; to test this function a relatively simple repetitive task must be carried out as swiftly as possible. The test may take the form of copying a page of digits or crossing out a series of horizontal lines. Older subjects perform poorly on these tests whether they call for some or no cognitive skill. The decline in function begins at approximately age 40 years and is rapid. The 70-year-old completes only about half as many items as does the 30-year-old. A related test calls for the subject to write as slowly as possible. Young men but not young women have this skill. Again, there is a very sharp decrease in performance with age. It appears that the older individual operates within a fixed and narrow range of speed in performing tasks. The failure to accelerate may be a deliberate attempt to avoid error in the presence of impaired cognition; the inability to perform more slowly than is customary may reflect a loss of cortical inhibition in the old person.

SUGGESTED READING

Botwinick J, Storandt M: *Memory, Related Functions and Age*. Springfield, Ill, Charles C Thomas, Publisher, 1974.

Corso JF: *Aging Sensory Systems and Perceptions*. New York, Praeger Publishers, 1981.

Feinberg I: Changes in sleep cycle patterns with age. *J Psychiatr Res* 1974; 10:283–306.

Kales JD: Aging and Sleep, in Goldman R, Rockstein M (eds): *The Physiology and Pathology of Human Aging*. New York, Academic Press, 1975, pp 187–202.

Kausler FH: Cognition and Aging, in Shadden BB: *Communication Behavior and Aging*. Baltimore, Williams & Wilkins Co, 1988.

Kent S: Can drugs halt memory loss? *Geriatrics* 1981; 36:34–41.

Miles LE, Dement WC: Sleep and Aging. *Sleep* 1980; 3:119–220.

Thompson LW, Marsh GP: Psychophysiological studies of aging, in Eisdorfer C, Lawton MP (eds): *The Psychology of Adult Development and Aging*. Washington, DC, American Psychological Association, 1973, pp 112–148.

12

Nutrition and Drug Metabolism

NUTRITION AND AGING

All too little is presently known about the special dietary requirements of the older population. Nonetheless this segment of the population is inclined or is persuaded to purchase disproportionate amounts of expensive dietary supplements such as vitamin and mineral preparations.

It is well established that caloric restriction prolongs the maturation period and the life span in experimental animals, but this may not have direct bearing on the question of nutrition of the already elderly or old person. However, obesity is a risk factor for several diseases that shorten the life span, and this condition is prevalent in our abundant society. Increases in body fat content are "usual" aging changes in this country, but this is clearly more life-style induced than age related. Although the majority live in the presence of abundance, malnutrition is common in all age groups in this country; it takes the form of inadequate intake of specific nutrients and caloric overnutrition arising from a diet rich in convenience foods and calories.

Several factors tend to make the older person susceptible to suboptimal nutrition. Food becomes less attractive to the older person for several reasons. Loss of the senses of smell and taste robs food of much of its pleasure. The age-related changes in esophageal motility and competence of the lower esophageal sphincter can make mealtimes uncomfortable. Especially for the older person living alone, the chore of shopping and cooking seems hardly worthwhile, and less nutritious, prepared foods such as TV dinners are substituted. Loss of teeth without adequate replacement makes chewing difficult, and this together with a reduced flow of saliva leads the older person to select soft foods, often carbohydrates, rather than the more demanding meats, fresh vegetables, and salads. Too often the cost of a well-balanced, nutritious diet is prohibitive to the older person.

The first criterion for an adequate diet is that it should provide enough calories to support the body's metabolism without producing obesity. It is important to consider two facets of metabolism separately. First is the basal metabolic rate, which falls progressively with age after full growth has been achieved and reflects the slow reduction in lean body mass. The second facet is the calories needed to support activity. With aging, and especially with retirement, there is likely to be a substantial decrease in physical activity (see Fig 5–7). The requirement for "activity calories" differs widely from one individual to another. Although there are tables that specify the energy cost of everyday tasks and leisure activities, these are an imperfect basis with which to assess the caloric requirements of old people; with age, the "machinery of work" becomes less efficient largely because of the stiffening of joints, the increased internal work involved in muscle contraction, and impaired muscular coordination. This lowered efficiency is more marked as the work that is undertaken becomes more strenuous. In general, an old person has a decreased caloric requirement. The advice is often given that intake should be reduced by 15% from ages 45 to 65 years and thereafter by 10% each decade. However, this may be poor advice; the alternative approach might be to maintain activity at as high a level as possible and adjust the diet so as to maintain the lean body mass. As will be seen, the present advice relative to bone mass is, by a combination of dietary supplementation and exercise, to maintain this as far as possible at the youthful level. It is possible that some part of the old-age morbidity might be reduced if lean body mass were to be similarly maintained.

To remain in nitrogen balance, the older person requires a higher protein intake than that generally proposed as adequate (0.8 g of protein per day per kilogram of body weight). This increased protein requirement may be due to either impaired absorption or to an impaired utilization of the protein. Although there is insufficient information available about the metabolic aspect, it appears more likely that the problem lies there rather than at the absorptive level, although the reverse may be true in the achlorhydric individual.

Some old people display an impaired fat absorption sometimes attributed to inadequate secretion of pancreatic lipase. Some animal studies have also suggested that there may be age-related changes in chylomicron formation. Although fats are important to make the diet more palatable and are necessary as a source of essential fatty acids and as a vehicle for the fat soluble vitamins, wise advice would appear to be to reduce fat intake so that no more than 25% of calories come from this source.

Information about vitamin metabolism in older people is insufficient to propose any age-specific recommended dietary allowances. Analysis of typical diets of old people suggests that requirements are being met but there is a reduced margin of safety so that deficiencies can more easily arise when the old person is sick or disabled.

The critical factor is the quality of the diet. Common problems are inadequate amounts of meat in the diet, which may lead to shortage of B group vitamins (especially B_{12}), an inadequate intake of fruit and vegetables, and a deficiency of vitamin C. There is a well-marked reduction in the formation of vitamin D in the skin in older people, even when they are exposed to adequate light. This impairment becomes even more marked in individuals who are indoors for a large part of the time. Further the renal conversion of the vitamin to its active form is reduced as kidney mass falls.

Calcium absorption falls with age, and it is apparent that the recommended daily intake of 800 mg is insufficient in older members of either sex but especially in postmenopausal women. Supplementation to a level at least 50% higher together with steps to ensure adequate vitamin D intake are necessary to protect against the two common bone diseases of the aging—osteoporosis and osteomalacia. Body stores of iron tend to be low, and reduced gastric acidity may also lead to an iron deficiency. Trace minerals are at a marginal level even in the ample diet of young people so that reduction in total food intake may lead to deficiency. Of the trace elements, zinc is of particular interest since zinc deficiency has been postulated as involved in the loss of olfaction and taste, and in impotence.

Fiber is an important component of the diet, and in the old, intake may be deliberately reduced because of difficulties in chewing and swallowing. Pureed vegetables and fruits can ensure an adequate intake while circumventing this problem.

Loss of taste sensation leads many to increase their intake of salt and refined sugar above the already excessively high levels of the common diet.

Finally, mention should be made of an item of alimentation not usually considered as part of nutrition, namely water. Many old people electively reduce water intake because of incontinence or difficulty getting to a bathroom. Others may have problems serving their own needs for fluids. Dehydration of even minor extents has undesirable effects including constipation. Special attention to an adequate daily intake is necessary in those taking diuretics; some attention may also be necessary to potassium intake in such cases.

DRUGS AND THE AGED

Older people consume more prescription and over the counter drugs per capita than do younger people, and it is estimated that over 25% of all drug sales are to the 12% of the population over the age of 65 years. It has been reported that the average older person purchases 13 prescription drugs per year. Drug consumption is higher among the institutionalized aged than among those in open society. The incidence of adverse side effects to drugs (per drug taken) is twice as high as in the young. In part this may be due to interactions between multiple drugs being taken for multiple diseases, but these adverse reactions may also be the result of the altered physiology of the old.

The action of drugs may be considered in two ways, one the pharmacokinetics and the other the pharmacodynamics. Pharmacokinetics is concerned with the absorption, transport, distribution, metabolism (biotransformation), and elimination of the drug; pharmacodynamics addresses the interaction of the drug with a receptor site through which its effect on the target cell is produced.

Absorption

In old individuals, reduced blood flow to the gut, changes in the absorptive epithelium (probably more theoretical than actual), reduced motility, and delayed gastric emptying all alter the absorption of drugs given by the oral route.

A reduction in the acidity of the gastric contents, which is a small change in the absence of atrophic gastritis and is largely confined to men, affects the solubility of some drugs and, in the case of weakly acidic drugs, reduces absorption by increasing the degree of ionization.

Perhaps the commonest group of drugs taken by old people is antacids, and these exacerbate the effects of lowered gastric acidity. The absorption of several common drugs is affected by concurrent use of antacids; for example, digoxin and tetracycline are absorbed less well; the absorption of levodopa is increased.

Transport in the Blood

The extent to which a drug is free to distribute throughout the body components is dependent on the extent to which it is bound to plasma protein and red blood cells. The concentration of plasma albumin is lower in the old; hence, more drugs that are normally bound to albumin are in the free, available form. In general, the binding of drugs to red blood cells does not change with age. This makes sense because red blood cells are constantly replaced and thus do not reflect the age of the individual.

These two factors, absorption and transport, are the primary determinants of the quantity of drug available to the body. Drug effects are dependent on concentration and the time the drug is present (the area under the curve of concentration plotted against time.) A useful characterization of the pharmacokinetics is the half-life ($t^1/_2$) of the drug within the body compartments:

$$t^1/_2 = 0.693 \times \frac{\text{volume of distribution}}{\text{clearance}}$$

Volume of Distribution

With age, the total amount of body water becomes a smaller fraction of the body weight, so that drugs that distribute in total body water become relatively more concentrated if administered on a body weight basis. Also, the increased body fat content of the older person leads to the accumulation and extended presence of drugs that are very soluble in lipids.

Clearance

Clearance of a drug refers to two basic processes: (1) the biotransformation of the drug into an active or inactive product and (2) the elimination of the drug from the body.

The process of biotransformation commonly occurs in the liver and involves the microsomal enzyme systems for hydrolysis, oxidation, or conjugation of the drug. The reduction in liver mass and blood flow with age slows this process. In addition, with age the microsomal enzyme systems are less readily induced.

Drugs are eliminated from the body by the gut (sometimes following hepatic secretion into the bile), by the skin in sweat, by the lungs if volatile, or by the kidney. Of these routes, the last is the major avenue for most drugs. The decrease in the number of nephrons with the associated reduction in the glomerular filtration rate and renal perfusion leads to a persistence within the body of drugs that are simply filtered or that are also actively secreted by the tubular epithelium. The age-related reduction in the ability to concentrate the urine or to excrete osmotically uncommitted ("free") water may also be a pertinent factor in drug elimination.

Glomerular filtration is commonly evaluated by the clearance of creatinine, and the absolute rate of creatinine excretion correlates with the lean body mass. In Chapter 6, a formula was given for prediction of the glomerular filtration rate at various ages, and this provides a guide for dosage of drugs that are cleared by the kidney. While less than a perfect guide, it is superior to schedules of dosage based on body weight or surface area.

Volatile drugs eliminated by the lungs are retained longer in the old body as a consequence of the increased functional residual capacity (i.e., reduced ventilatory coefficient) and the poorer matching of ventilation and perfusion.

Pharmacodynamics

The activity of many drugs changes in the older individual independently of the amount of drug presented to the target tissue. These changes may be attributed to (1) alterations in the interaction between the drug and its receptor site or (2) alterations in postreceptor mechanisms including the capability of the tissue to perform the appropriate response.

In a young person, atropine increases the heart rate as much as 50% above the initial value; in the old, the change is usually slight. This may be explained by a reduced number of muscarinic receptors in the old heart. In general, the old show less response to drugs that have a stimulant effect on the central nervous system (CNS) (e.g., amphetamine), while the response to depressants (e.g., chlorpromazine) is enhanced. Barbiturates, which are depressants in the young, tend to be stimulants in the old. This effect may be explained in terms of differential aging of the target centers (perhaps differential loss of receptor sites). The response to sympathomimetic drugs changes with age as a result of preferential loss of β-receptors or even the conversion of β to α receptors.

An example of limitation of response at the target tissue is provided by the reaction of aortic smooth muscle to norepinephrine. As the aorta ages, it becomes less compliant, and the contraction response is reduced. Likewise the relaxation response to isoproteronol is much reduced. The β-blocking agent propranolol reduces cardiac output, but in the old, the effect is reduced in proportion with the lower pretreatment value.

Compliance

The incidence of adverse drug effects in the old is probably due in a majority of cases to noncompliance with dosage schedules or failure to inform the prescribing physician of other drugs being used. The individual may not be aware of the hazards of alcohol when taken, for example, in association with a central nervous system depressant or the effects that smoking may have on biotransformation processes. Common, simple over-the-counter preparations such as aspirin or decongestants can produce significant interactions with prescription drugs. Compliance is more difficult in the old than the young for several reasons, not least of which is that the old person may be taking four or five drugs each day. A failing memory may lead to a dose being missed or repeated; failing vision may interfere with reading labels or recognizing the color of tablets; failing hearing may lead to a misunderstanding of verbal instructions.

SUGGESTED READING

Nutrition

Brody JA: Prospects for an aging population. *Nature* 1985; 315:463–466.

Chernoff R, Lipschitz DA: Aging and Nutrition. *Compr Ther* 1985; 11:29–34.

Exton-Smith AN, Caird FI (eds): *Metabolic and Nutritional Disorders in the Elderly*. Chicago, Year Book Medical Publishers, 1980.

Harper AE: Dietary guidelines for the elderly. *Geriatrics* 1981; 36:34–43.

Kohrs MB: A rational diet for the elderly. *Am J Clin Nutr* 1982; 36:788–795.

Rockstein M, Sussman ML: *Nutrition, Longevity and Aging*. New York, Academic Press, 1976.

Schneider EL, Vining EM, Hadley EC, et al: Recommended dietary allowances and the health of the elderly. *N Eng J Med* 1986; 314:157–160.

Drugs

Brandell ME, Brandell RR, Hult R: Pharmacology and the aging system, in Shadden BB (ed): *Communication Behavior and Aging*. Williams & Wilkins Co, Baltimore, 1988.

Fisher CR: Differences by age group in health care spending. *Health Care Finance Rev* 1980; 1:65–90.

Krupa LR, Vener AM: Hazards of drug use among the elderly. *Gerontologist* 1979; 19:90–95.

Platt D: Pharmacotherapy and old age. *Triangle* 1986; 23:43–52.

13

Biological Age, Functional Age, the Aging Worker

In Chapter 1 the concept of successful and unsuccessful aging was introduced to accommodate the increasing diversity of functional levels which appears during the aging process. From this consideration arose a second concept, that of "biological age," which describes for a particular function the age at which the observed value is "usually" seen (see Fig 1–4).

The function plotted on the ordinate need not be a physiologic measure, and the equivalent concept of "functional age" has been used in the description of psychological age, work task capacity, or more general capacity for functioning in society. In the broader context, "functional age" is very much involved in the issues of recruitment and retention of older persons in the work force: this is mentioned later.

If we confine our attention to changing physiologic function, we can extend the significance of our estimation of biologic age to the idea of how far an individual has progressed toward that level of impaired function that is incompatible with survival (Fig 13–1). In other words, biologic age is not a measure of how long one has lived, but rather how far toward death one has proceeded. In fact, biologic age could be an assessment of remaining life span, or time before "eugeric" death as it was earlier defined.

The idea of biologic age has been used extensively at the opposite pole of the life span in the study of growth and development. Here some well-defined markers of stages of development are available—progress of calcification, eruption of teeth, onset of puberty, for example. These markers are sufficiently regular to make "precocious"

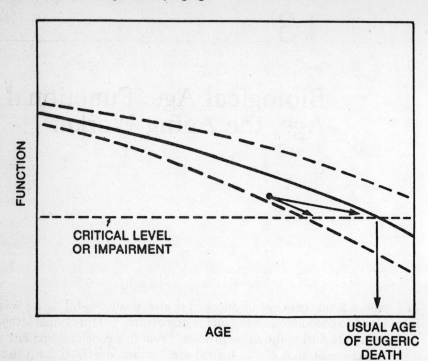

FIG 13–1.
The decline of function with age and its relation to time of "eugeric" death. The arrows indicate the way in which intervention may change the rate of decline toward the critical level of impairment.

or "delayed" development meaningful terms. No such clear markers exist for the aging process.

Attempts have been made to develop a battery of measurements that might be used for estimating biologic age; the criteria that have been applied in the selection of tests for such a battery include the following:

1. The function tested should show a marked change with age so that there is significant alteration over a reasonable short span of years, for example, 3 to 5 years.
2. The tests chosen should cover as broad a spectrum of functional systems as possible.
3. The tests should be performed with as little disturbance of the subject as possible.
4. The performance of the test should not be dependent on the motivation of the subject.

TABLE 13–1.
Measures of Biologic Age

Variable	Correlation With Age
1. Skin deformability	+0.604
2. Systolic blood pressure	+0.519
3. Vital capacity	−0.402
4. Hand grip strength	−0.323
5. Reaction time	+0.488
6. Vibratory sensitivity	−0.537
7. Visual acuity	−0.423
8. Threshold of hearing at 4,000 Hz	−0.596
9. Level of serum cholesterol	+0.234

5. The tests should be suitable for screening large numbers of people.

Most aging changes begin at early middle age—40 to 50 years. Thus, it is probably futile to attempt to develop a battery of tests that cover the span from young adulthood to extreme old age: it is more profitable to consider particularly the years from age 40 years onward. A battery of tests was developed by Hollingsworth and colleagues in 1965 for examining the survivors in Hiroshima. Nine functions were selected. These are listed in Table 13–1 together with the correlation of the function with age. Hollingsworth studied more than 400 individuals and found a high degree of correlation between chronological age and an index of physiologic age derived from these measurements. However, where such a high correlation between chronological age and biologic or physiologic age exists, one might question the usefulness of such a scale except for estimating the age of individuals who lack the customary evidence of time since birth. Of the nine measures included in Table 13–1, probably no more than three could be regarded as survival related.

Borkan and Norris (1980) published a procedure for the assessment of biologic age that uses a similar battery of tests. They used data from the longitudinal study conducted by the National Institute on Aging. Having established the regression of a particular measurement on age, they subtracted the predicted value for that measurement from that observed in an individual and then converted the residual to a z-score. The z-scores, either positive (arbitrarily taken as indicating a biologic age greater than chronological) or negative, were then plotted as a profile. Such a profile might show that a person is younger than his years in, say, cardiovascular function but has "overaged" in psychomotor function. In other words, this procedure examines the "harmony" of the aging process and serves to identify functions that might be targeted for intervention so as to optimize function toward survival.

If the objective of assessing biologic age is to establish a prediction of "remaining life span," the functions selected for inclusion in the test battery must be those that are critically related to survival. In the field of intensive care medicine, an appropriate battery of tests has been devised, the APACHE system (*acute physiology and chronic health evaluation*), which evaluates the degree of deviation of a patient's physiologic test results from what is seen as the desirable norm. Serial measurements then allow evaluation of the effectiveness of interventions. This system, with modification, could be extremely useful in the geriatric field. However, there would be a downside to such an index of "predicted survival" in that it might be abused as a form of triage for opportunities or benefits.

The abolition of a mandatory retirement age brings the issue of functional age into sharp focus. Just as with biologic or physiologic age, the problem is what should appear on the ordinate as the measured function—should this be an index derived from a series of laboratory tests or should it be some measure of on-the-job performance? The conflict between chronological age and functional age has been exposed in debates over the mandatory retirement of public safety workers based solely on chronological age. Physiologists have in some cases been able to devise tests that appear to evaluate performance in the critical components of assigned tasks and so provide a "functional age" for a specific job performance.

THE AGING WORKER

During the past 100 years while life expectancy has been growing apace, participation of older persons in the labor force has consistently declined. A hundred years ago, 68% of those over the age of 65 years continued in employment; by 1950, the figure was 45%, and in 1980 it was 20%. Despite recent changes in policy, the trend continues; older persons continue to leave the work force in increasing numbers and at earlier ages. Often retirement is elective, but perhaps equally often it is the result of being unable to compete successfully for available employment opportunities. The headlong pace of technological development places a premium on the ability of the worker to be retrained in new tasks. The employer is able to find ample reasons for preferring the younger employee. Some of these reasons include the following physiologic realities:

1. The young person is capable of greater durations and intensities of physical work.
2. The process of learning is slowed in the older worker, calling for longer periods for retraining.
3. Memory for complex sequential tasks is poor in many older persons.
4. Older persons cope less well with suboptimal environmental conditions, e.g., of temperature, lighting, etc.

While these are realities, their significance relative to employment may be limited. For example, measurements of maximal oxygen uptake are a useful way of assessing the collective efficiency of the several steps in the chain of oxygen acquisition and utilization. However, such measurements are divorced from the real-life situation in that maximal rates are sustained for only a very few minutes. In the working place, even in situations of perceived hard work, the energy expenditure over the course of a working shift is very much lower. Industrial practice recognizes the desirability of the worker not becoming excessively fatigued during the working period, and data from several industries have suggested that a mean energy expenditure of about 30% of the maximum over an 8-hour period will allow the worker to complete the shift without a level of fatigue that would call for a significant recovery period.

It has been shown that there is a linear relationship between the energy output (measured as oxygen uptake) and the logarithm of the time for which that level of energy output can be sustained. The plot shown in Figure 13–2 indicates that the maximum VO_2 can be sustained for 4 to 5 minutes, and an uptake one third of maximal can be sustained for a continuous period of 8 hours. If the work load exceeds this limit, then either the duration of the work shift must be shortened or the work must be undertaken intermittently with intervening rest periods so that the average oxygen consumption of work and rest falls within 30% of the maximum limit of VO_2.

Between the ages of 25 and 65 years there is typically a falloff in maximum VO_2 of a third or more. If the older worker is not to finish his work period significantly more fatigued than his younger workmate performing the same task, either the total shift must be shortened or rest breaks provided.

These energy considerations should not be taken to imply that the older worker is necessarily less productive. In many tasks, experience increases skill so that a job can be accomplished with a lower expenditure of energy (in which case the rest requirement would be reduced) or with a greater speed so that production over the reduced working period would more nearly match that of the younger worker over the longer period.

Rather similar considerations apply to vigilance tasks which with automation of industrial processes, are becoming more numerous and important. The factor that differentiates old and young is a shorter time to fatigue; in the nonfatigued state, they are equally effective provided attention is paid to the needs of the older person for higher levels of illumination and more intense auditory signals.

The learning impairment that might be present in older people is dependent on the speed at which material is presented and so calls for

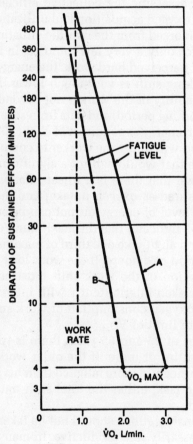

FIG 13–2.
The relationship between oxygen consumption and duration of effort for a healthy young man (*A*) and a healthy elderly man (*B*). The vertical *dashed* line is set at an oxygen consumption rate of one third of the maximum VO₂ for the younger individual.

changed patterns of training. Similarly, memory impairments can be minimized by presenting tasks in manageable segments.

Performance at all ages is affected by adverse thermal environments. Accident rates, for example, show almost no age dependence on ambient temperatures below 21°C. At 26°C, the accident rate for 35 year olds is twice that at 21°C, whereas for 60 year olds, it is four times higher. The older worker needs higher levels of illumination at the workplace and adapts less well to different levels of lighting. Good safety practice calls for optimization of the environment for all workers; conditions suitable for the older worker will work to the benefit of the younger also.

Another aspect of the retirement question is the reduction in level of activity that all too often it entails. It may be an invitation to "hypokinetic disease" and progressive life-shortening morbidity. It would be in society's best interest to encourage continued participation in work by older people rather than to strive to provide levels of support that will tempt them to the park bench.

SUGGESTED READING

Atchley RC: *Social Forces and Aging: An Introduction to Social Gerontology.* Belmont, Calif, Wadsworth Publishing Co, 1988.

Birren JE: The concept of functional age: Theoretical background. *Hum Dev* 1969; 12:214–215.

Borkan GA, Norris AH: Assessment of biological age using a profile of physical parameters. *J Gerontol* 1980; 35:177–184.

Comfort A: *Aging: The Biology of Senescence.* New York, Elsevier North-Holland, Inc, 1978, pp 299–312.

Hollingsworth JW, Hashizume A, Jablon S: Correlations between tests of aging in Hiroshima subjects—an attempt to define "physiologic age." *Yale J Biol Med* 1965; 38:11–26.

Rowe JW, Kahn RL: Human aging—usual and successful. *Science* 1987: 237:143–149.

Salthouse TA: Functional Age, in Birren JE, Robinson PK, Livingston JE (eds): *Age, Health and Employment.* Englewood Cliffs, NJ, Prentice-Hall, 1987.

Tobin JD: Physiological Indices of Aging, in Danon D, Shock NW, Marois N (eds): *Aging: A Challenge to Science and Social Policy,* vol 1: Biology. New York, Oxford University Press, 1981.

Index